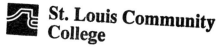

WOMEN
COMICS
IN THE

REVISED & UPDATED

Chelsea House Publishers

WOMEN
IN THE
COMICS

REVISED & UPDATED

MAURICE HORN

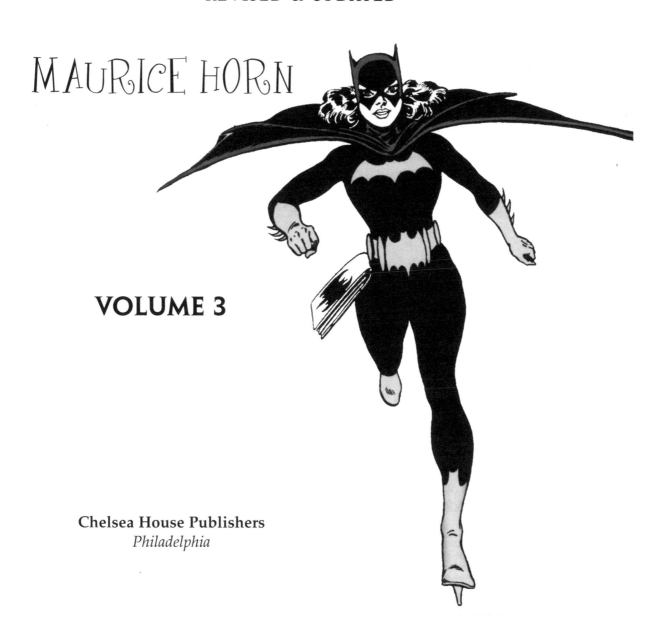

VOLUME 3

Chelsea House Publishers
Philadelphia

Printed and bound in the Hashemite Kingdom of Jordan.

First printing
1 3 5 7 9 8 6 4 2

Library of Congress Cataloging-in-Publication Data
applied for

ISBN 0-7910-5913-8

Chelsea House Publishers
1974 Sproul Road, Suite 400
Broomall, PA 19008-0914

The Chelsea House World Wide Web address is
www.chelseahouse.com

Acknowledgments

Many people have helped with documentation, suggestions, and advice during the planning and realization of this book. It is a pleasure to express my sincere appreciation to: Bill Blackbeard, Jerry Iger, Burne Hogarth, Dorothy Herscher, Jerry Muller, John Knight, Susan Lusk, and Maryvonne Fortier; a special note of thanks to Richard Marschall for his invaluable assistance in researching the illustrations for this book.

Acknowledgment is also extended to King Features Syndicate, the Chicago Tribune-New York News Syndicate, NEA Service, Marvel Comics Group, DC Comics Inc., ERB, Inc., United Feature Syndicate, McNaught Syndicate, Universal Press Syndicate, Editions du Lombard, Le Terrain Vague, Milano Libri, and the National Cartoonists Society.

I wish to honor the memory of my former publisher, the late Harold Steinberg, whose well-documented interest in the subject provided the original impetus for this book.

I wish further to thank the many people who have been of help with this updated edition of the work, and more particularly John Lent, Bill Crouch, Mary Beth Calhoun, Dominique Petitfaux, Annie Baron-Carvais, Hongying Liu-Lengyel, Francisco Tadeo Juan, Giulio Cesare Cuccolini, and Bill Janocha. Special thanks should also go to Cathy Haibach of Tribune Media Services and to Brendan Burford of King Features Syndicate for their kind cooperation on this project.

Finally I wish to thank my publisher, Philip Cohen, and all the people at Chelsea House for their support and assistance.

Also by the Author

A History of the Comic Strip (with Pierre Couperie), 1968
75 Years of the Comics, 1971
Comics of the American West, 1977
Sex in the Comics, 1985
100 Years of American Newspaper Comics, 1996
The World Encyclopedia of Comics (ed.), revised and updated, 1999
The World Encyclopedia of Cartoons (ed.), revised and updated, 2000

Contents

VOLUME 1

1   Introduction

15   Preface to the Second Edition

17   **Chapter One:** The First Draft **1897-1910**

35   **Chapter Two:** A Place of One's Own **1910-1919**

48   **Chapter Three:** Working Girls and Flappers **1920-1929**

75   **Chapter Four:** The Royal Road to Adventure **1930-1939**

VOLUME 2

113   **Chapter Five:** The Fighting Forties **1940-1949**

139   **Chapter Six:** The Frolicsome Fifties **1950-1959**

160   **Chapter Seven:** You've Come a Long Way, Baby **1960-1975**

192   **Chapter Eight:** Whatever You Can Do I Can Do Better **1976-1989**

VOLUME 3

217   **Chapter Nine:** No Millennium in Sight **1990-2000**

          Color Section: after page 240

241   **Chapter Ten:** A Century of Women in the Comics: A Progress (and Regress) Report

270   **Bibliography**

272   **A Sampler of Women Cartoonists**

281   **Index**

NO MILLENNIUM IN SIGHT
1990–2000

9

In her 1993 book *A Century of Women Cartoonists* Trina Robbins claims that, "there were ten strips drawn by women in the daily newspapers in 1942," while in 1992 she avers, "I have counted exactly four strips by women cartoonists" (while actually naming five of them). This slight lapse in arithmetic aside, Robbins is comparing the proverbial apples and oranges here. First there were twice as many daily newspapers in America published at that time than there are today, while the number of nationally syndicated strips was three times larger (about 600 then compared to fewer than 200 now). Furthermore 1942 was the first full year of wartime for the United States, with many cartoonists and their assistants being drafted into the armed forces, which forced syndicates to hire female replacements by default (the Rosie the Riveter syndrome): thus Gladys Parker, for instance, came to draw *Flyin' Jenny* for a few months in that period.

While the situation in the 1990s was not as black as Robbins portrayed it, it was still far from ideal, or even fair. It is a fact that most of the comic strips originated in this decade came, as in the preceding ones, from the pens of male cartoonists, a sad circumstance that is not likely to end soon for a variety of reasons, some of which are examined in this and the final chapter. Yet some syndicates at least tried to distribute the creations of female cartoonists: three such in this decade have been Madeline Brogan's *The First Lady*, Barbara Dale's *The Stanley Family,* and Kathy Le Mieux's *Lyttle Women*. All three of them centered on women and family, and all three of them were short-lived. And finally there is the case of *Suburban Cowgirls,* which was drawn by Ed Colley, a man, and written by Janet Alfieri, a woman, making the strip the perfect representative of equal gender rights in the funnies; unfortunately it too did not last long.

Some women have fared better in this decade, however. One of them is Barbara Brandon, the daughter of noted black cartoonist Brumsic Brandon Jr. (the creator of *Luther*) and the first African-American woman cartoonist to be nationally syndicated with *Where I'm Coming From.* Her themes are not only those of racism and social alienation emphasized by her father, but also those closer to women's concerns, such as sexism, single motherhood, and women's equality. By showing only the faces and hands of her revolving cast of African-American women characters talking about their problems against a blank background, she is able to evoke the stark realities daily confronting her protagonists.

Unlike Brandon whose weekly feature has been a success almost from the start, Jan Eliot had to, in her own words, "hang in there" for some years. After failing to click with two semiautobiographical strips in the 1970s and 1980s, the third time proved the charm when *Stone Soup* (a reworking of her earlier efforts) was picked up for national syndication in 1995. It features a widowed working mother, Val Stone, trying to cope simultaneously with a job and her two daughters, teenage Holly and nine-year-old Alix (originally modeled on the author's own daughters, now grown to adulthood). They all live under the same roof with Val's sister Joan (also a working single mom) and her toddler son Max. Grandmother Stone rounds out the extended family. Their neighbor (and Joan's sometime date) Wally also drops in with some home-cooked lasagna (yes, some men in the funnies have indeed learned to cook). The feature is finely drawn and wittily scripted; as Lynn Johnston wrote, "I expect Jan and her work to enhance the lives of comics-loving families everywhere for a long, long time!"

Male cartoonists too came up with some worthwhile feminine creations in this decade. In *Mama's Boyz* Jerry Craft introduced "Mama" Pauline Porter, an African-American widow who owned a bookstore and had to cope with her two teenage boys as well as with some weird customers. In *Outland* (described by the author as a country "for those who don't fit in,") Berke Breathed of *Bloom County* fame had as his main protagonist a little black girl named Ronald-Ann Smith who had sought refuge there from all the sorrows and miseries of urban ghetto life. In the idyllic setting of *Liberty Meadows*, in contrast, Frank Cho placed Brandy, who could talk to the animals, as a kind of sexier version of Doctor Doolittle, as well as someone who brought out the animal in her male cohorts. In this decade the newspaper strip cleared one remaining taboo with *Color Blind,* described by its syndicate as "a comic by Orrin Brewster about a loving interracial family."

The last worthwhile entry in the feminine iconography of the comic pages came at the very tail end of the decade. In March 1999 Tony Cochran's *Agnes* debuted in a handful of newspapers and soared to the top in a few months: the titular character is a little girl with a big head and big dreams living on the edge of poverty in a trailer with her grandmother. As the author stated, "Agnes is a kind of indomitable spirit. She is poor but not stupid." Finally let us mention *Moose* which in recent years underwent a title change to *Moose and Molly,* in recognition of the equal role played by the long-suffering wife of America's most celebrated layabout.

Finally liberation of sorts also came to some of the old, established favorites of the funny pages. Mary Worth has managed an apartment building, along with other forms of gainful employment, while continuing to provide her own brand of wisdom to all and sundry; Lois (the female half of *Hi and Lois*) sells real estate (not too successfully); and the sacrosanct male precincts of Camp Swampy (in the *Beetle Bailey* strip) have been invaded by the tough-talking, tough-acting Sgt. Louise Lugg who can run circles around the befuddled Sgt. Snorkel. Even Blondie, while not shedding her apron, is now running a catering business in partnership with her best friend Tootsie.

On the comic book front more superpowered heroines were added to the mix at the major publishing companies, most of them retreads from earlier incarnations. Black Canary, for instance, had been a tough justice-fighting judo expert and motorcyclist whose powers varied from one adventure to the next. In the 1990s she was turned into a straight superheroine whose physical appearance varied from coltish to punkish, and whose exploits were cut short by lack of reader interest.

Two other revenants from bygone times were not actually super-heroines but rather supermagicians that had been created in the wake of Lee Falk's successful *Mandrake the Magician*. One was Zatanna who was the daughter of another magician, Zatara, and who had apparently sprung full-blown in the 1960s before disappearing before the decade was out. As revived thirty years later, her magic seemed to pertain more to technology than to old-time occultism and wizardry. Weirdest of all was Doctor Fate who had started life as a man way back in the early 1940s and who used a crystal ball and could fly. For some unaccountable reason the good doctor underwent a sex change and emerged as a sensitive liberal do-gooder who used her powers for the betterment of society and the protection of the environment to the enraged howls of protest from the mostly male readers.

Original superwomen creations came from smaller, independent publishers. There was an African-American warrior woman who was fighting for freedom in an America of the future gone haywire; she was perhaps too cleverly named Martha Washington. Another gimmick was supplied by Lady Justice who in actuality was not one woman but several, taking turns in donning the magic blindfold that transformed them into instruments of (what else?) imminent and expeditive justice. While not *stricto sensu* a superwoman, Barb Wire, a tough-as-nails bounty hunter of some unnamed future, should also be added to the mix because of her superhuman abilities.

As her name indicates, Ghost was already dead when she sprang to life (so to speak) in her own comic book. As befits a visitor from the beyond, she only fought evil menaces from the netherworld. Doing her one better has been Death herself. In previous gambits of the sort, the Grim Reaper had almost uniformly been embodied by men, as witness Fredric March in *Death Takes a Holiday* or Brad Pitt in *Meet Joe Black*. In this version Death was a young girl whose vernal appearance belied her lethal powers.

While newfangled comic book heroines have been relatively plentiful, if transient, in the final decade of the past century, the crop of adolescent girls coming of age in this period has been disappointingly (or happily, depending on the point of view) scarce, and just as evanescent. The only creation worthy of note in this field has been *Barbie,* based on the famous doll. Written and drawn by a number of women, it only lasted for the first half of the decade.

Television has always provided lucrative fodder for comic book publishers, and the 1990s proved no exception to this rule, and some of the more interesting comic book heroines were literally plucked out of existing TV shows, all of them sporting qualifiers that said it all. First came *Sabrina, the Teenage Witch,* whose comic book incarnation turned out to be a little more lighthearted than its small screen counterpart. It was soon followed by *Xena: Warrior Princess,* which starred a strong woman (in every sense of the word) who not only could outfight, outrun, and outsmart any of her male opponents, but who was also a champ at archery, swordplay, and javelin throwing.

All of the foregoing creations hewed close to their TV models; *Buffy, the Vampire Slayer,* whose creator, Joss Whedon, is a comic book fan of long standing, notably departed from the norm. Buffy, in Whedon's words, "was larger than life and she fought monsters," and therefore was a natural for comic book heroics. She was given a supporting cast of weird characters, and unlike the retail business she did on television, in comic books she fought hordes of demons and armies of phantom riders in the course of a single episode.

The nineties have not been kind to women working in comic books. All of the titles devoted to the work of women creators and launched with so much expectation in the seventies were gone well before the end of the decade, with the oldest of them, *Wimmin's Comix* (changed from *Wimmen's Comix,* to get the "men" out of the title), making its final bow in 1992. The situation was alleviated somewhat with more and more women cartoonists opting to either self-publish or have their works issued by small-press publishers and distributed through the direct market, therefore maintaining a feminist presence, however slight, on the comic book scene. This is the case of Canadian-born Julie Doucet's *Dirty Plotte,* among others, an autobiographical title that Roger Sabin characterized as "a mix of sleaze and dark surrealism," but one that nonetheless "somehow exudes a *joie de vivre*"; of Coleen Doran's *A Distant Soil,* about a female emissary of hope and renewal from a faraway planet; and of Roberta Gregory's *Naughty Bits,* directly inspired by the author's own daily experiences in a variety of settings.

A special instance is provided by Aline Kominsky-Crumb. As the wife of legendary cartoonist Robert Crumb, her works have always enjoyed wider circulation than those of most of her female colleagues. She is currently recounting (in humorous fashion, as "Blabette") her experiences in France, where she moved with her husband in 1990. Her autobiographical reminiscences are painfully comprehensive, chronicling even the couple's often hair-raising marital disputes (as the 1995 documentary film *Crumb* had also done).

The 1990s brought a retrenchment in comics production in Europe;

yet a few worthwhile feminine creations came from the inspired pens of cartoonists, men and women, in this period. French woman cartoonist Chantal Montellier created in Julie Bristol an investigating reporter who fought for social justice along with feminist causes. In *Vae Victis* (Latin for "Woe to the Vanquished," the motto of the Roman legions) Jean-Yves Mitton brought to the comics pages the legendary Briton warrior-queen Bodicea who fought the invading Roman armies in the first century B.C.

The Romans came in for more knocks in Germany where Franziska Becker originated Feminax and Walkuriax as a feminist answer to the French Astérix and Obélix. Those two symbolically named women fought the legions of the Roman Empire to a standstill almost by themselves in this parody of Hollywood epics.

True to form Japanese cartoonists kept turning out comic books starring young girls in heroic situations, most of them by female cartoonists. Particularly notable in this respect was Naoko Takeuchi's *Sailor Moon,* which was aimed at a teenage girl audience but rapidly become a favorite of male readers as well after a highly successful series of TV animated cartoons was later released. Fourteen-year-old Usagi Tsukino is a high school student who thanks to a magic tiara is transformed into Sailor Moon, a superheroine whose mission it is to save the Earth from demons and monsters. "The attraction of *Sailor Moon,*" Fred Patten wrote in *The World Encyclopedia of Cartoons,* "is that it enables young girls to fantasize themselves as powerful as their brothers' macho superheroes, without losing any of their femininity."

The 1990s also saw the emergence of comics as a full-fledged narrative form on the continent of Africa, which until then had had little use for them. Tanzania checked in with *Anti Bwalo,* a very successful comic strip about female relationships by Martha Gellege who, Leif Packalén informs us in *Comics in the Development of Africa,* is "one of the very few African female comics artists." In neighboring Kenya, Frank Odoi, probably Africa's best-known cartoonist, came up with *Just like a Woman,* a story about a typical male chauvinist set straight by two female cops.

On the southern tip of the continent, in the Republic of South Africa, three foreign-born cartoonists originated *Madam and Eve,* a very funny strip about a white matron, Gwen Anderson ("Madam") and her tart-tongued black maid Eve Sisulu. The always pithy and often acidulous exchanges between the two women constitute the core of the feature and aim, in the words of John A. Lent, "to make South Africans laugh at themselves, while also making them squirm a bit."

At the dawn of the new millennium the picture may not look as bright as might have been hoped for women in the comics. Yet it is certainly better than it had been at any time during the more than one hundred years that the medium has been around. Certainly as far as American newspaper strips are concerned the depiction of women, their representation, and their concerns have received unprecedented coverage, some of it in the last couple of years alone. *Editor & Publisher*'s 1999 Syndicate Directory lists no fewer than 30 strips distributed by the major syndicates in which women or girls either are the leads or share equal billing with their male counterparts, from *Agnes* to *Zenon—Girl of the 21st Century.* This puts them almost at parity with features having males as the exclusive leads. Each silver lining seems to have a cloud hanging over it, however, and American comic books on the other hand appear for the most part to have permanently regressed to an adolescent (male) stage, with big-muscled males and big-busted females occupying almost the entire scene.

There have been some hopeful signs from foreign countries in this respect, as documented by the examples cited in the course of the present chapter. So while the millennium may not yet be in sight for the women on the funny pages, there are signs and portents that bode well for favorable developments in the coming decades—no cause perhaps for breaking out the champagne, but a modest sparkling wine might not be out of order.

Granny, Gary Kopervas ("Out on a Limb"). Another feisty oldster came to the comics pages when the tough-acting Granny started to dispense her own brand of wisdom to all and sundry in 1999. A Mary Worth she isn't, is the best that can be said for her. © King Features Syndicate.

Brandy, Frank Cho ("Liberty Meadows"). Frank Cho's creation first appeared in the University of Maryland campus newspaper and later in comic books before being picked up for syndication. The star of the strip is the toothsome Brandy who shares the spotlight with a host of funny animals, including a jumping frog, a midget bear, and a chauvinist pig that turns out to be a real swine (or vice versa). © Creators Syndicate.

The women of "Where I'm Coming From," Barbara Brandon. Since 1991 cartoonist Brandon has used her rotating cast of seven African-American women in her weekly newspaper strip to comment on everyday life in the inner-city ghetto, but also to tackle the more universal themes of life, love, and death. She is particularly intent on discrediting the stereotypes attaching to black culture in general and to African-American women in particular. © Universal Press Syndicate.

Agnes, Tony Cochran. For some unexplained reason the year 1999 was particularly fertile in resourceful little girls living with a single female parent. Agnes is a savvy five-year-old who dwells on the edge of poverty in a tiny mobile home with her grandmother. A funny, yet touching feature, "Agnes" has taken its place among the newspaper strips to watch. © Creators Syndicate.

Betty, Gary Delainey and Gerry Rasmussen. Canadian-born Delainey and Rasmussen had worked together on comic strip projects since their University of Alberta days. In 1991 they succeeded in having "Betty," which their syndicate describes (perhaps tongue-in-cheek) as "a celebration of today's real woman," gain international distribution in North America and several European countries. A pudgy, middle-aged office worker, Betty can hold her own in the office, at home, and on the golf course. © United Feature Syndicate.

Blondie, Dean Young and Denis Lebrun. The more things change . . . "Blondie" may have gone through several changes of personnel since its inception, and its titular heroine may now run a business, but things are likely to remain pretty much the same in this highly popular strip. Why change a winning formula, the authors seem to imply with a wink. © King Features Syndicate.

Val Stone, Jan Eliot ("Stone Soup"). An ensemble piece about several generations of women, the strip revolves around Val Stone, a widowed working mother, and her extended family (made up of her mother, daughters, sister, and nephew) all living together. The interaction between the women and occasional male characters constitute the heart of the matter in this funny and thoughtful strip originated in 1995. © Universal Press Syndicate.

Maxine and Darlene, Ed Colley and Janet Alfieri ("Suburban Cowgirls"). Maxine ("Max") Marshall, a single mother of two, and Darlene Dillon, a childless married woman, were two working women in their thirties. The strip, which ran from 1990 to 1998 and was written by a woman, dealt in a humorous vein with the difficulty of holding on to relationships, the problems of the workplace, and life in suburbia in general. © Tribune Media Services.

Death, Neil Gaiman and Dave McKean. Following a long tradition in Western art dating back to the Middle Ages, comic books in turn tried to give us a pictorial representation of Death, starting in 1990. In this particular instance she was portrayed as a pretty teenage girl wearing jeans and eye shadow. © DC Comics.

Zenon—Girl of the 21st Century, Roger Bollen and Marilyn Sadler. Zenon (perhaps named for the ancient Greek philosopher) was a space heroine of the coming century, as indicated by the subtitle. Her adventures started in a 1996 children's novel, later adapted into a Disney movie. She came to the comics pages in 1999, and by 2000 she was gone, having managed to span two centuries in one short year. © Tribune Media Services.

Lola, Steve Dickenson and Todd Clark. The year of the grandmother was without a doubt 1999, with Lola joining the ranks of curmudgeonly oldsters.
© Tribune Media Services.

Eve, Madeline Brogan ("The First Lady"). Eve was "the first lady," since the scene of this strip was Earth after the Fall. There she was surrounded by friendly animals and tended to her family: husband Adam, sons Cain and Abel, and her wholly uncanonical daughter Ivy. This unconventional and winsome strip only lasted a couple of years (1993-1995).
© Tribune Media Services.

Xena, Warrior Princess. Xena was a six-foot-tall warrior princess who fought for the rights of the downtrodden. She was described as "a kind of she-hunky leather queen who sails through the air like Bruce Lee" and could grab arrows in midflight, among other feats of valor. Her muscular adventures have taken place on television since 1995, and were adapted to comic books the following year. © Topps Comics.

Elvira, *Mistress of the Dark*, José Villagran. The tongue-in-cheek adventures of the popular TV horror show hostess came to comic books in 1993. © Claypool Comics.

Buffy, the Vampire Slayer. Joss Whedon had been a long-time comic book fan when he wrote the screenplay for the 1992 *Buffy, the Vampire Slayer* movie, later a successful TV series. It is therefore no surprise that the character of the fearless nemesis of all malevolent night creatures would be transferred to the comics pages (in 1997). © Twentieth-Century-Fox.

Marcy, Robb Armstrong ("JumpStart"). Described by the syndicate editors as "a reflection of today's middle-class America," the African-American middle-class family depicted here consists of Joe Cobb, a police officer; his wife Marcy, a nurse; and their infant daughter Sunny (born after the feature's inception). Marcy's juggling of a career and parenthood provides much of the appeal in this charming comic strip. "JumpStart" has met with well-deserved success since its debut in 1990.
© United Feature Syndicate.

Jazmine, Aaron McGruder ("The Boondocks").
Jazmine is a girl growing up with other children of
color in a predominantly white suburb. This interracial
strip, launched in 1998, according to its syndicate, is
"hip-hop, and it's now." © Universal Press Syndicate.

Gwen Anderson and Eve Sisulu, Harry Dugmore,
Stephen Francis, and Rico Schacheri ("Madam and Eve").
The most popular strip in South Africa happens to star
two strong-minded women, one black, one white, one an
upscale dowager, the other her maid, but both equally
assertive and neither of them shy in expressing their
opinions. This satirical feature met with instant success
after it began in 1993. © Rapid Phase Entertainment.

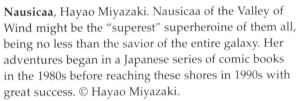

Nausicaa, Hayao Miyazaki. Nausicaa of the Valley of
Wind might be the "superest" superheroine of them all,
being no less than the savior of the entire galaxy. Her
adventures began in a Japanese series of comic books
in the 1980s before reaching these shores in 1990s with
great success. © Hayao Miyazaki.

Anti Bwalo, Martha Gellege. A warm and wise woman, Anti Bwalo is everybody's favorite aunt in this charming comic strip in the Swahili language created by woman cartoonist Martha Gellege in the mid-1990s. © Martha Gellege.

Judette Camion, Jeanne Puchol and Anne Baraou. A self-mocking and warm "plain Jane," Judette has known a number of contretemps and misadventures at work and at play since her first appearance in 1997. © Casterman.

The girls of "Naughty Bits," Roberta Gregory. In her comic book feature provocatively titled "Naughty Bits," Gregory uses a recurring cast of women characters to comment on various facts of life, many culled from personal experience. © Roberta Gregory.

Tank Girl. Jamie Hewlett. Tank Girl, a female skinhead always spoiling for a fight in her stolen tank, began her obnoxious career in 1990 in the pages of the British comics magazine *Deadline*. The character proved popular enough to be later adapted to American comic books, as well as to a 1995 movie. © Jamie Hewlett and Alan Martin.

Dirty Plotte, Julie Doucet. Despite her squalid existence and her foul language, Dirty Plotte (whose life experiences are loosely based on the author's own) exudes a certain optimism and winsomeness that belie the underlying cynicism of most of the storylines. She originally appeared in her eponymous comic book in 1991.
© Julie Doucet.

Durga, ("Tales of Durga"). This is a direct comic book representation of the Hindu goddess of myth and religion. A many-armed supernatural being who comes down to earth when the world is in danger, she came down to comic books in 1991 in this English-language version. © Amar Chitra Katha.

Bela, Jagjit Uppal and Pramod Brahmania
("Bahadur and Bela"). This Indian comic book
started in the mid-1970s, but the character of
Bela, at first the subservient assistant to the hero
Bahadur, only attained parity with her male
companion in the early 1990s. © Indrajal Comics.

Belinda Blinks, Charles William Kahles
("Hairbreadth Harry"). © Jessie Kahles Straut.

Mary-Jane, Richard Felton Outcault
("Buster Brown").

Mary-Jane, Richard Felton Outcault
("Buster Brown").

Bécassine, Caumery (Maurice Languereau) and
J.P. Pinchon. © Gauthier-Languereau.

Miss Peachtree, Ed Carey ("Simon Simple").

5. LEANDER (wildly): "Lulu, what does this mean? Where is he? Where is that man who dares avow his love? And you, YOU utter no word of protest. Where is he, I say? Nay, nay, don't hide him. It shall be his life or mine!"

3. LULU: "Leander, how dare you! I WILL go. You don't own me YET. Come on, Charley; come on, Lieutenant."
CHARLEY: "You will be safe with US, I guarantee, Lulu. Come on, Lieutenant."

Lulu, F.M. Howarth ("Lulu and Leander").

Lady Bountiful, Gene Carr ("Lady Bountiful").

Dixie Dugan, John Striebel and J.P. McEvoy.
© McNaught Syndicate.

Fritzi Ritz, Ernie Bushmiller. © United Feature Syndicate.

Jane Arden, Jack McGuire. © Register and
Tribune Syndicate.

Sally, Jack Callahan ("Freddie the Sheik"). © King
Features Syndicate.

Toots, Jimmy Murphy ("Toots and Casper").
© King Features Syndicate.

Rosie, George McManus ("Rosie's Beau").
© King Features Syndicate.

Tillie the Toiler, Russ Westover. © King Features
Syndicate.

The Stenog, A.E. Hayward
("Somebody's Stenog").
© Ledger Syndicate.

Flapper Fanny, Gladys Parker. © NEA Service.

Mamma Katzenjammer, Rudolph Dirks ("The
Katzenjammer Kids"). © King Features Syndicate.

Connie, Frank Godwin. © Ledger Syndicate.

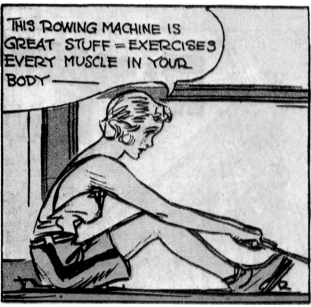

Mrs. Newlywed, George McManus ("The Newlyweds and Their Baby").

Fluffy Ruffles, Wallace Morgan.

Hildegard Hamhocker, T.K. Ryan ("Tumbleweeds"). © King Features Syndicate.

Phyllis, Gene Carr.

Jennie Dare, Russell Keaton ("Flyin' Jenny").
© Bell Syndicate.

Minnie Ha-Cha, Allen Saunders and Elmer Woggon ("Big Chief Wahoo"). © Field Newspaper Syndicate.

Betty Boop, Bud Counihan. © King Features Syndicate.

The Flame, Will Gould ("Red Barry"). © King
Features Syndicate.

Rota, William Ritt and Clarence Gray ("Brick Bradford"). © King Features Syndicate.

Molly Day, Charles Schmidt and Eddie Sullivan ("Radio Patrol"). © King Features Syndicate.

Wonder Woman, William Marston and H. G. Peter. © DC Comics Inc.

Aleta, Harold Foster ("Prince Valiant"). © King
Features Syndicate.

Sheena, Robert Webb ("Sheena, Queen of the Jungle"). © S. M. Iger.

Myra North, Charles Coll. © NEA Service.

Lil de Vrille, Alex Raymond ("Jungle Jim").
© King Features Syndicate.

Sala, Lee Falk and Ray Moore ("The Phantom").
© King Features Syndicate.

Tess Trueheart, Chester Gould ("Dick Tracy").
© Chicago Tribune-New York News Syndicate.

Mary Worth, Ken Ernst and Allen Saunders.
© Field Newspaper Syndicate.

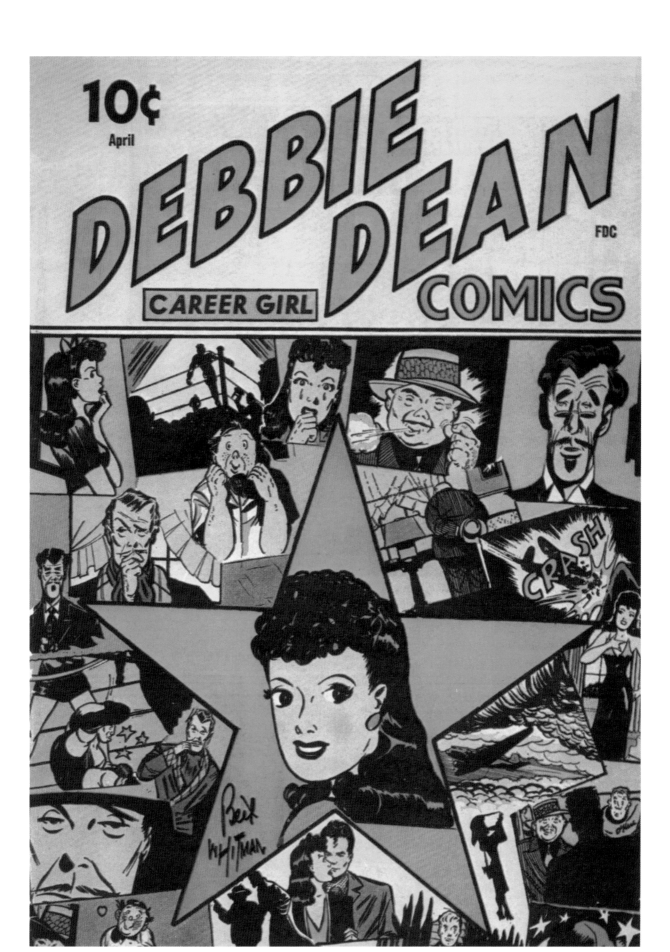

Debbie Dean, Bert Whitman. © New York Post Syndicate.

Blondie, Chic Young. © King Features Syndicate.

Miss Fury, Tarpe Mills ("Black Fury"). © Bell Syndicate.

Scarlet O'Neil, Russell Stamm. © Chicago Times Syndicate.

Witch Hazel, Burne Hogarth ("Miracle Jones"). © United Features Syndicate.

Jodelle, Guy Pellaert.
© Le Terrain Vague.

Ms. Marvel, Jim Mooney and Joe Sinnott. © Marvel Comics Group.

Gwen, Stan Lee and John Romita ("Spider-Man"). © Marvel Comics Group.

Red Sonja, Frank Thorne. © Marvel Comics Group.

Gale, Zack Mosley ("Smilin' Jack"). © Chicago Tribune-New York News Syndicate.

Spider-Woman, from model sheet. © Marvel Comics Group.

Flamingo, Burne Hogarth ("Drago"). © Burne Hogarth.

Isis, Mike Vosburg and Vince Colletta. © Filmation Associates.

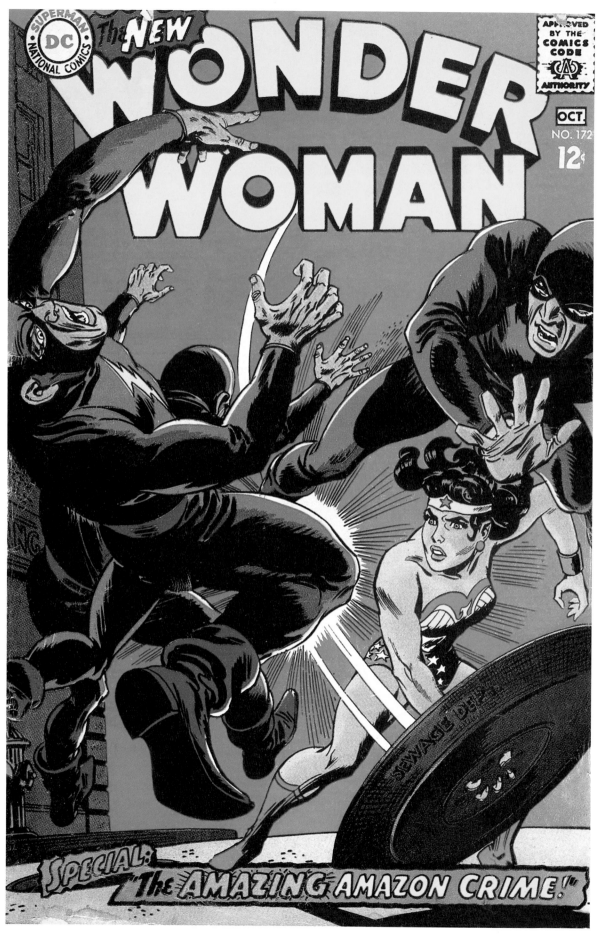

Wonder Woman. © DC Comics.

Spider-Woman. © Marvel Comics.

La Diva et le Kriegspiel, Annie Goetzinger. © Annie Goetzinger.

Barbarella, Jean-Claude Forest. © J.C. Forest.

Marina Seminova, Hugo Pratt ("Corto Maltese"). © Hugo Pratt.

Buffy, the Vampire Slayer. © Twentieth Century-Fox.

Annie, Leonard Starr. © Tribune Media Services.

Nungalla and Jungalla, Mary & Elizabeth Durack. © Sunday Telegraph (Sydney).

Jill Bioskop, Enki Bilal ("La Femme-Piège").
© Dargaud.

Six Chix, Anne Telnaes. © King Features Syndicate.

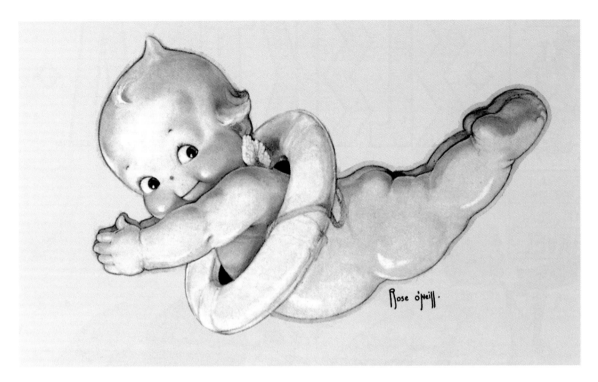

Rose O'Neill, Kewpie advertisement.

Nausicaa of the Valley of Wind,
Hayao Miyazaki.

Cover of Wimmen's Comix. © Wimmen's Comix.

Kitty Pryde. © Marvel Comics.

Adèle Blanc-Sec, Jacques Tardi.
© Casterman.

Angelica ("The Rugrats").   © Nickelodeon.

One Big Happy, Rick Detorie.   © Creators Syndicate.

Agnes, Tony Cochran.   © Creators Syndicate.

"MOMMY, DID YOU EVER FALL IN
LOVE WITH ANYBODY?"

The Family Circus, Bil Keane.   © Bil Keane.

Cathy, Cathy Guisewite.   © Universal Press Syndicate.

Marge and Lisa Simpson, Matt Groening ("The Simpsons").
© Universal Press Syndicate.

A CENTURY OF WOMEN IN THE COMICS: A PROGRESS (AND REGRESS) REPORT

American books and articles that have dealt with the topic of women working in the field of comics have always done so from the exclusive and parochial perspective of the United States. Yet there is a larger—much larger—story begging to be told on that subject, and that's what this chapter will attempt to do.

It is a little-known fact that among the early European pioneers who helped shape the narrative form that came to be called the comics, there was a woman. Marie Duval was born Isabelle Emilie de Tessier in France and later moved to England where she eventually hooked up with Charles Henry Ross, creator in 1867 of *Ally Sloper,* which some British historians of the medium regard as the first bona fide comic strip. As stated by Denis Gifford in *The World Encyclopedia of Comics,* "Helping him with the inking, and taking over completely once the series was established, was Marie Duval, a French teenager whose real name was Emilie de Tessier, otherwise known as Mrs. Charles Henry Ross." Her drawings graced many a cover of *Ally Sloper's Half-Holiday* in particular.

It would take a long time before another woman cartoonist would make it into British comics. She was Mary Tourtel, née Caldwell, who had embarked on a career as a children's book illustrator at the end of the 19th century. In 1920 she originated in the pages of the (London) *Daily Express* the extremely successful *Rupert the Bear,* which was to survive the death of its creator by several decades. Another early woman comics artist in the English-speaking world was the Australian Cecilia May Gibbs, a children's book author and illustrator, who in 1925 adapted one of her creations, *Gumnut Babies,* into a Sunday comics page titled *Bib and Bub,* which ran until 1967.

The comics, in the meantime, had been exploding all over the American map, principally in San Francisco, Chicago, Philadelphia, and New York.

Most of the practitioners were male, but a surprising number of women also showed up on the comics pages of American newspapers in the early years of the 20th century, mainly turning out features about either young children or debutantes. There was Kate Carew who created *The Angel Child* about a young girl who was anything but; Inez Townsend, who did *Gretchen Gratz* without the use of speech balloons, a throwback to earlier times; Jean Mohr, a prolific purveyor of comic fun with such titles as *Easy Edgar* and *Sallie Slick and her Surprising Aunt Amelia*; and many others.

The names of these trailblazing artists are nearly forgotten today; but others have left a more permanent trace. Grace Wiederseim (who after her second marriage was to sign Grace Drayton) began her long career at the beginning of the 20th century, notably drawing *Toodles* (a conventional kid strip), *Dolly Drake and Bobby Blake* (more kids), and *The Turr'ble Tales of Kaptin Kiddo* (about a small boy and his fantasy adventures, a comic page that was also spelled more conventionally on occasion). As all these titles indicate, she drew, in a style that was overly cute and mannered, features intended chiefly for young children.

The most celebrated woman cartoonist of the period, however, was Rose O'Neill, whose creation, *The Kewpies,* has endured lasting fame to this day. These cupid-like and cherubic-looking characters invaded the pages of magazines, and later of newspapers, in the form of comics stories, pages, panels, and strips, from 1905 to 1919, when O'Neill closed down her features as a sign of mourning for the Allied dead of World War I. Her silence was to continue for more than 15 years.

Female cartoonists were almost exclusively confined to kid's and women's features, and the 1920s proved no exception. This was the era of the flapper, and while some flapper strips, such as *Betty* and *Dumb Dora,* were created by men, most were the work of women. There was *Flapper Fanny* by Ethel Hays, a cartoonist of great range who also turned out Sunday pages on the same theme of flaming girlhood; *Flapper Fanny* was later taken over by Gladys Parker, who in the next decade would create a variation on the type with *Mopsy.* Dot Cochran originated the charming and short-lived *Me and My Boyfriend,* among others. The most prolific practitioner of the genre was Virginia Clark (a.k.a. Virginia Huget), who in the course of a long career that lasted well into the 1950s provided variations on this single theme with such confections as *Babs in Society, Campus Capers,* and *Molly the Manicure Girl.*

Then came the Thirties and the Depression, and the mood turned somber, even in the funnies. Yet women cartoonists still were shackled to earlier stereotypes such as Gladys Parker's *Mopsy,* Ethel Hays's *Marianne,* and Dorothy Urfer's *Annibelle.* When a woman, Martha Orr, tried to reflect the temper of the times with *Apple Mary,* about an elderly widow forced to sell apples to provide for herself and her crippled grandson Denny, her original creation lasted for only five years, and the feature was eventually taken over by two men, Allen Saunders and Ken Ernst, while Apple Mary turned into Mary Worth with a classier wardrobe and a brighter outlook.

One subject that was thought to be suitable grist for women cartoonists' mills was the depiction of adorable little girls. Veteran cartoonist Fanny Cory tried to turn those to advantage with gritty tales of orphaned young girls making it in the cruel world of adults through spunk and wits (Babe Bunting, Little Miss Muffet). Of a more conventional mold was Marge Henderson's resourceful and spirited Little Lulu, who would later enjoy a long run in comic books. Cute animals and even cuter little creatures were also staples. Edwina Dumm's *Tippie* (about a sprightly mutt) and Grace Drayton's *The Pussycat Princess* (which dealt with a kingdom full of lovable kittens) fit that bill; but they couldn't hold a candle in the cuteness department to *The Kewpies* that Rose O'Neill brought back to the comics pages in 1935. And in 1937 a black woman artist, Jackie Ormes, started her comic strip career with *Torchy Brown,* exclusively published in the black press.

The fledgling comic book industry employed women cartoonists as early as the 1930s, but most of them chose to disguise their gender. Thus Cecilia Paddock Munson signed "Pad," Ramona Patenaude was known as "Pat," while June Mills became Tarpe Mills of *Black Fury* fame. In the same vein Dahlia Messick had to change her first name to Dale before being able (in 1940) to sell *Brenda Starr* to the editors of the newly minted "comic book magazine" insert in the Sunday supplement of the *Chicago Tribune.*

During World War II some new female artists were hired to replace those male cartoonists who had been drafted: thus Ann Brewster, Peggy Zangele, and Ruth Geller, among others, came briefly to illustrate superhero or war stories, but mostly they were asked to take over so-called girl's comics that had hitherto been drawn by men. Similarly the newspaper comics pages received an infusion of new feminine blood in the persons of Gladys Parker (on *Flyin' Jenny*) and Mabel Odin Burvik, who replaced her husband Coulton Waugh for a couple of years on *Dickie Dare*. A special case is that of Neysa McMein who drew *Deathless Deer* with scripts by *Chicago Tribune* heiress Alicia Patterson.

Teenage girl strips proliferated in the 1940s; while most were done by men, they did help start the careers of Hilda Terry, who created *It's a Girl's Life* (later changed to *Teena*), and Marty Links, the author of *Bobby Sox* (a.k.a. *Emmy Lou*). Virginia Clark topped her long career when in that same period she took over yet one more teenage girl strip, *Oh, Diana,* from its creator Don Flowers. *Susie Q. Smith,* a panel in the same vein, was also drawn by a woman, Linda Walter, with texts by husband Jerry Walter. Dale Conner, who had carried on *Apple Mary* for a few years, came up with *Ayer Lane,* an action strip written by her husband Herb Ulrey.

The decade was also a golden age for women in comic books: with romance and teen comics flourishing on the newsstands they had no trouble finding employment. Artists like Ruth Atkinson, Ann Brewster, and Valerie Barclay worked on such titles as *Millie the Model, Patsy Walker,* and *Young Love*. When working on action titles, however, they had to change to male names: such was the case for Hazel Marten, who used the pen name Sean (not Scott, as erroneously stated elsewhere) Fleming on the western *Nevada Jones.*

Next to the United States, no country in the 1940s was as hospitable to female comics artists as Australia. Working for newspapers there were, among others, the sisters Mary and Elizabeth Durack, who authored the beautiful *Nungalla and Jungalla* Sunday page, based on Aborigine legends; Kath O'Brien who created *Wanda the War Girl,* whose eponymous heroine battled Japanese invaders and German spies in World War II; and Moira Bertram (signing "Bert") who came up with Jo, featuring the adventures of a black-tressed dancer who used a magic cape as her weapon. Bertram later went on to a prolific career in Aussie comic books, with such titles as *Jo and her Magic Cape* (a continuation of her newspaper strip), *The Red Prince,* and *Flameman* to her credit.

Unlike the preceding decade, the 1950s proved unfriendly to women seeking employment as artists in either comic strips or comic books. This was the time of stay-at-home moms and *Father Knows Best.* No notable female cartoonist emerged in the newspaper pages, and comic books proved no more receptive: the women artists employed there worked almost exclusively as colorists or in production work. (The lone exception was Ramona Fradon who drew the second-string *Aquaman* at DC for a good part of this period.) The situation was no better in other English-speaking countries. In England only Evelyn Flinders, who had had a distinguished 20-year career in illustration, surfaced at the beginning of the decade as a major presence in the field, drawing *The Silent Three,* based on a series of juvenile novels, and other comics for schoolgirl's magazines until she went back to illustration in 1959. In Australia Mollie Horseman drew *Pam,* a long-lasting Sunday page starring an attractive blonde teenager, which had been conceived by another woman, Jean Cullen. But that was about all for this uneventful decade (which for all practical purposes can be said to have spilled over into the early part of the 1960s).

The 1960s (especially during the latter half) and the 1970s were a different matter altogether. In comic books the change became apparent from the earliest years of the period. Ramona Fradon finally graduated to drawing the company's major titles, including *Superman, Batman,* and *Plastic Man.* The same was true for Marie Severin, who had languished for years in Marvel's production department, and in 1966 started illustrating *Doctor Strange, Sub-Mariner,* and *The Cat,* among others. The trend unfortunately did not last long, and by the 1970s the major comic book companies, under pressure of their overwhelmingly male readership of "fanboys" clamoring for more and more overmuscled superheroes, regressed back to their old ways.

In newspaper strips the reverse proved true: the decade began with a whimper and ended with a bang. Cathy Guisewite came up with *Cathy* in 1976 and Lynn Johnston created *For Better or for Worse* in 1979 (their work is discussed in a previous chapter), two trailblazing features that are still running today with great success. They paved the way for the great flowering of women on the comic pages that took place in the following decades.

The most notable development came not from the already established fields of comics, but from the so-called underground comix that sprang up from the grass roots in the early 1960s: it was in the underground press that Trina Robbins, for instance, got her start. The women undergrounders soon became upset by the treatment they received from their male counterparts and in the early 1970s issued their own comic books, the most enduring of which was *Wimmin's Comix.* In its 20-year existence it showcased the work of, among others, Lee Marrs, Sharon Rudahl, Roberta Gregory, and Melinda Gebbie. The 1970s also witnessed the emergence of the alternative press whereby comics authors could self-publish their own creations and have them distributed through comic book shops: Wendy Pini, with the help of her husband Richard, launched her long-running series of *Elfquest* comic books in just this way.

That same 20-year period was equally favorable to British women in the comic book field: Jennifer Robertson, for instance, illustrated many original stories for the English publisher of *Classics Illustrated.* British newspapers also opened their pages to up-and-coming women cartoonists. Pat Tourret and Jenny Butterworth created *Tiffany Jones* in the 1960s; and since the 1970s Rosemary ("Posy") Simmonds had her weekly comics featured in the respected newspaper *The Guardian.* The British were not long in establishing their own underground tradition, but they seemed to keep women at arm's length. Not so the Australians, who had started their own brand of alternative press in the late 1960s: it was in this venue that such female cartoonists as Pat Woolley (a transplanted American) and Tina Amor made themselves known.

In the last two decades of the 20th century the trend accelerated, with an increasing number of women joining the rank of newspaper cartoonists. While some of their creations did not survive long (*The First Lady, Lyttle Women, The Stanley Family,* for instance) others, such as Barbara Brandon, Sylvia Hollander, and Lynda Barry have become firmly established in the comics pages. They have been joined in more recent years by Jan Eliot (*Stone Soup*), Hilary Price (*Rhymes with Oranges*), and June Brigman (*Brenda Starr,* succeeding Ramona Fradon). Women still constitute a small minority among comic strip creators, but their numbers keep slowly increasing, a good omen for the new century.

The situation also somewhat improved as far as mainline comic books were concerned. There was an attempt to revive the romance comics genre, as we have seen in the preceding chapter, and while it proved ephemeral, it did give work to a number of women artists and writers, including Barb Rausch, Amanda Connor, Barbara Slate, and the inevitable Trina Robbins. No woman in this period secured a permanent position drawing one of the major superhero or fantasy titles where the money is, however, with the lone exception of Mary Wilshire on *Red Sonja.*

In contrast to the two or three major companies in the field, the independent publishers proved more hospitable to women creators: Donna Barr's *The Desert Peach* (about General Rommel's fictitious gay brother in World War II) and Coleen Doran's *A Distant Soil,* among others, saw light of print there. Some women creators chose to go the self-publishing route (either solo or as a collective), as was the case of Diane Noomin, Debbie Drechsler, Mary Fleener, Carol Lay, the British Myra Hancock, and Quebec-born Julie Doucet.

Even some comic book publishers are beginning to come around to a policy of at least partial affirmative action. *Dignifying Science,* a nonfiction book in comics format extolling the discoveries of female scientists that came out at the end of 1999, employed eleven women cartoonists (including Donna Barr, Ramona Fradon, and Marie Severin), one for each of its subjects. And in January 2000 King Features started offering a daily panel and Sunday page for every day in the week (and in rotation on Sundays), showcasing the work of six different female cartoonists (Isabella Bannerman, Margaret Shulock, Rina Piccolo, Ann Telnaes, Kathryn LeMieux, and Stephanie Piro, in that order) . The feature called (feminists will shudder) *Six Chix* has been described by the syndicate's Jay Kennedy as "a new concept in syndication," in which "the cartoons all have a female point of view." Limited as they are, these initiatives may well prove a harbinger of things to come.

Women cartoonists in the non-English-speaking world were relatively slow to assert themselves prior to the World War II era, even in girls' publications. In France, aside from a few isolated cases (mostly wives assisting their cartoonist husbands), there were practically no women in comics prior to World War II. After the war a few women started work in girls' magazines, notably Manon Iessel, Janine Lay, and Colette Pattinger, who illustrated stories for such publications as *Fillette*. Martine Berthelemy, who had debuted in women's magazines, later went on to draw for the weekly *Journal de Mickey* in all genres (adventure, fantasy and science-fiction, costume epics, etc.) for over 20 years from the mid-1950s to the mid-1970s.

The real breakthrough came with Claire Bretécher who entered the field in the early 1960s. She later produced such winning series as *Les Gnan-Gnan* (a kid strip) and the humorous *Les Naufragés* ("The Castaways," with texts by Raoul Cauvin). Her greatest success came in 1969 with *Cellulite,* a hilarious comic strip about a homely spinster princess; she followed up with *Les Frustrés* ("The Frustrated Ones"), a weekly page of social and political commentary which she has been contributing to the prestigious newsweekly *Le Nouvel Observateur* since 1975.

After Bretécher came the flood. Probably the best-known female cartoonist is Annie Goetzinger, who started her long career in the late 1970s. Her most notable productions have been *Félina* (discussed in an earlier chapter); *Aurore,* a biography of feminist 19th-century author George Sand; and a number of loosely related period pieces taking place in the Europe of early 20th-century, all of them centered around strong female protagonists. An even more powerful feminist (and politically radical) message is contained in Chantal Montellier's comic strip series, chief among them the mystery-shrouded *Julie Bristol* and her biography of Virginia Woolf. Florence Cestac is the polar opposite of the socially engaged Montellier: her forte is burlesque, notably in her long-running family strip *Les Déblok* (on which she succeeded another woman cartoonist, Sophie Hérout). For her part Jeanne Puchol created with scriptwriter Anne Baraou the slice-of-life *Judette Camion,* about an ordinary French woman. Among other women cartoonists in France who became noted in the last decade, mention should be made of Isabelle Dethan, Claire Wendling, and Anne Baltus.

Italy hasn't been as rich in feminine talent, but it still managed to produce a few notable women cartoonists. As early as 1942 Lina Buffolente began her longlasting and prolific career with a series of humorous comic books. Very soon, however, she specialized in Western tales (an unlikely calling for a woman, especially at the time), illustrating, among other stories in this vein, *Frisco Jim, Liberty Kid, Calamity Jane, Il Piccolo Ranger* ("The Little Ranger"), and an adaptation of the adventures of Buffalo Bill. In between she found time to draw *Furio Mascherato* ("The Masked Fury"), a superhero comic book; *Fiordistella,* a soap opera; and a number of mystery and adventure titles.

In a totally different register Grazia Nidasio created *Valentina Melaverde* in 1968, an engaging strip about a dreamy teenage girl, which is still being published to this day; while Anna Brandoli specialized in historical series set in medieval times with *La Strega* ("The Witch") and the uncompleted trilogy *I Testamenti di Sant'Ambrogio,* both of them starring female protagonists on the margins of society, one a woman reputed to be a sorceress, the other a Gypsy named Rebecca. Finally there is the phenomenon of *Diabolik,* created by the sisters Angela and Luciana Giussani, all about an amoral antihero whose criminal activities have remained highly popular with the Italian and international public since

1962, despite public outcry, denunciations from politicos, and even condemnation by the Catholic Church.

Paradoxically women cartoonists also flourished in Spain during the dictatorial rule of Francisco Franco, working for girl's magazines such as *Florita, Chicas,* and *Trinca.* Maria Pilar Sanchis particularly collaborated with most of those publications in the period extending from the late 1950s to the mid-1970s, specializing in fairy tales and romantic stories, as did Consuelo Arizmendi. The soap opera specialist, however, was unquestionably Carmen Barbara Geniés (signing simply "Barbara") who debuted at age 16 with *Carmencita,* and whose most noteworthy creation was *Mary Noticias,* which ran from 1960 to 1967. Maria Teresa Alzamora also drew fantasy tales and romantic stories, but she was one of the few female artists also capable of spinning adventure yarns: her most celebrated accomplishment in this domain was her drawing of *Pantera Negra,* one among the many Tarzan imitations that sprang up all over the globe in this period.

Even more paradoxically, the death of Franco and the restoration of democracy brought about the end of many of the escapist girl's magazines and an accordingly sharp reduction in the ranks of women cartoonists. The only memorable female comics creator to come out of the 1980s in Spain was Ana Miralles, who made her debut in the newly minted underground publications that emerged in the immediate post-Franco era. She later went commercial, and had her biggest success drawing *Eva Medusa,* a long-running thriller starring a femme fatale with preternatural powers, with scripts by Antonio Segura.

The situation in the rest of Europe does not look so rosy. In Germany, due to peculiar political and cultural reasons, comics never enjoyed the kind of public support they do in western Europe. Germany can boast of few comic strip authors of note, and even fewer women among their number. The only female name to stand out is that of Franziska Becker, who in her comic creations tackles feminine (and feminist) issues with a light touch and a great deal of humor, qualities that have made her, in Wolfgang Fuchs's words, "one of the most important female artists in Europe."

The only female cartoonist in northern Europe to have enjoyed great success for the not inconsiderable period of almost a half-century is Tove Jansson, who hails from tiny Finland. Her *Mumin* comic strip, based on her novels about a frolicsome family of trolls, has been running uninterrupted since 1954 and has been published at one time or another in 20 different languages.

Eastern Europe, where comics have been frowned upon for most of the post-World War II era, has accordingly produced few noteworthy women cartoonists: in this instance the most active of them has been Livia Rusz of Romania, who in the 1950s and early 1960s composed a number of comic strips based on folktales. In Russia, where under the Communist regime comics were banned outright for the longest time, it was only in the 1990s that practitioners of the medium started to emerge into the open: the only Russian woman cartoonist worthy of mention is Elena Uzhinova, who in style and tone can be related to the American undergrounders of the 1960s and 1970s.

Even more than the U.S., postwar Japan has been the country where female cartoonists have made the greatest strides on the way to gender equality. In a society as rigid and controlled as Japan, where women have long been considered second-class citizens, this is particularly remarkable and shows to what degree the little world of comics can sometimes be at variance with society at large. This quiet revolution was started by Machiko Hasegawa, who had been one of a very small number of women to have embarked on a cartooning career even before the war and who in 1946 created *Sazae-san*. A family strip of unusual humor and warmth, it enjoyed tremendous popularity in the pages of the Asahi newspapers in which it ran until 1975 (after which time it was reprinted in a series of 68 paperbacks). She later authored more strips featuring women, such as *Eipuron Obasan* ("Aunt Apron") and *Ijuwaru Basan* ("Stubborn Granny"), but none of them had nearly the same impact as her earlier creation. As Frederik Schodt declared, *Sazae-san*'s "success paved the way for a later rush of women artists in a field that had been completely dominated by men."

Many other women followed in Hasegawa's footsteps in subsequent decades, working mainly for girls' magazines. Among others there were Hideko Mizuno, who in *Fire!* ("Freedom!") chronicled the rise of a juvenile delinquent to rock stardom; Miyako Maki, the author of sexually liberated comic book stories; Moto Hagio, who was first to depict homosexual love in one of her comics; and Masako Watanabe, a prolific purveyor of romance comics. These four came collectively to be known as "the Magnificent 24-Year Group," because they were born in 1949 (in the Japanese calendar the year Showa 24).

Women working in Japanese comics in recent decades have been so numerous (much more numerous than in the U.S.) that only the most noteworthy can be mentioned here. Machiko Satonaka has been active in all genres, from romance to baseball stories; while Yumiko Oshima in her short stories has probed the most basic questions of human existence. Rumiko Takahashi is the creator of such popular stories (many translated abroad) as *Maison Ikkoku, Ranma 1/2,* and *Rumic World,* and is arguably the best-known Japanese female cartoonist in the U.S. We should also record the names of Ryoko Ikeda, the author of a fictional as well as monumental biography of Queen Marie-Antoinette in comic book form ("The Rose of Versailles"); Chikako Mitsuhashi, who has been working for comics publications and for newspapers with equal success; and Yoshiko Tsuchida, who specializes in gag strips, including the satirical *Tsuruhime Ja!* ("It's Princess Tsuru !"), about an ugly and nasty little princess, the bane of the royal castle. In more recent years special mention should be made of Naoko Takeuchi who in 1990 created the phenomenally successful *Sailor Moon.*

Across the Sea of Japan, China can also boast of a number of prominent women cartoonists. Wang Shuhui, who in all her adult life (except for the period of the Cultural Revolution from 1966 to 1976) has created a wealth of comic books blending classical painting and realistic images, is probably the most famous; her best-known work remains *Xi Xiang Ji* ("The West Chamber"), the adaptation of a celebrated Chinese novel.

Mao Yunzhi, who is a newspaper art editor as well as a comic strip artist; Liu Xiaoyuan, the author of a well-known husband-and-wife strip; Guo Shutian, who specializes in family strips; Liu Xinhua, author of a very funny strip about a perpetually disappointed suitor; and Lii Hongqun, an expert in self-contained gag strips, are all also worthy of mention in a field that is becoming more crowded with each passing year.

In India where comics and comics publishing houses are equally plentiful in a variety of languages (including English), there are practically no women cartoonists, except a handful, unfortunately anonymous, on the staff of the oldest comic book publisher in the country, India Book House. The Malaysian Cabai is probably the best-known woman cartoonist in South Asia. She writes and draws no fewer than three regular series, all of them featuring women and women's issues, in the Malay-language magazine *Gila-Gila*: *2's Kompeni* ("Two Is Company") is a gag strip about a bickering couple; *Joyah Sport* ("The Joy of Sport") is a tongue-in-cheek look at (what else?) women's sports; *Tiga Dara Pingitan* ("Three Well-Behaved Girls"), her most popular strip, is a humorous depiction of rural life from a woman's point of view.

In sorry conformity to their macho reputations, South American countries, for all their wealth of comic publications, have been almost bereft of women cartoonists. Only Yolanda Vargas in Mexico has asserted herself in this chauvinistic field when in the 1950s she took over the writing of the soap opera strip *Don Proverbio* created by Antonio Gutiérrez; she is better known, however, for having cofounded (with her husband Guillermo de la Parra) Editorial Argumentos, one of the most important publishers of Mexican comic magazines, specializing in soap operas (many of them written by Vargas). This in turn led to the establishment a few years later of the rival Publicaciones Herrerias which also gives work to a number of women, such as Maria Espinosa, Carmen Hernandez, and Josefina Diaz Herrera.

Arab comics only became established in the 1960s, and few women have become prominent in these countries. One can mention, however, the Lebanese Fatima Balabakki who, in *Rilhat Ibn Battuta*, spun a mock-heroic account of the fabled Arab traveler Ibn Battuta's journeyings, and Anissa Abdelrrahim of Morocco, author of the French-language *Juba II: Roi des Maures*, about the legendary ruler of Moorish Spain. While comic strip creation has come even later to the sub-Saharan countries of Africa, there are hopeful signs of the participation of women in this newly discovered medium: the Tanzanian Martha Gellege, the creator of a number of comic strips in Swahili, in addition to the popular *Anti Bwalo;* and Helena Motta of Mozambique, who has drawn a number of comic books in Portuguese, including a history of the Mozambican war of independence against Portugal, are two of the better-known women cartoonists on the African continent.

This necessarily brief global overview shows how much the subject is deserving of an in-depth treatment by a qualified researcher. In the meantime it is hoped that this will serve as a blueprint for further inquiry. The literature on the specific subject of women in the comics has expanded quite impressively since the time of the first edition of this work in 1977.

Marie Duval. "Ally Sloper." English cartoonist Charles Ross created "Ally Sloper" about an unsavory ne'er-do-well in 1867, but it was his assistant (and later wife) Marie Duval who actually assumed most of the drawing over the years. Here is an example from the first year of the feature.

Mary Tourtel, "Rupert the Bear." A children's book illustrator, Mary Tourtel came up with "Rupert" in 1920 for the London *Daily Express.* Rupert and his animal cohorts soon became such a hit with the readers of the newspaper that the feature has lasted to this day (with Tourtel drawing it until her retirement in 1935). © Daily Express.

A moment later the tiny airplane has landed and Rupert runs forward as an old friend gets out of it. "Why, surely you're the Golliwog that runs errands for Santa Claus, aren't you?" he cries. "Yes, I am, but who are you?" asks Golly. "You look like

Rupert of Nutwood but you're four sizes too small!" "Yes, I *am* Rupert," says the little bear. "I couldn't get in here while I was my right size." And he tells why he came and how the jumping men are squabbling with one another about their moves.

The Golliwog is evidently in a hurry and he marches off to the factory just as the manager appears again. "Hi, what are you up to?" says Golly. "Santa Claus is stocking up for his Christmas journeys and he hasn't yet received a single game of Halma

or Ludo or Tiddleywinks or . . . " "But I've just told you about the quarrelling counters and the jumping men," Rupert interrupts. "I told them what their squabbling means to other people, but they're so angry they won't listen to me!"

Rose O'Neill, "The Kewpies." O'Neill began her long career in 1896 and contributed countless illustrations to magazines and newspapers. The Kewpies, cupid-like characters who she claimed came to her in a dream, proved her most enduring creation, culminating in the celebrated Kewpie doll, the ultimate in cuteness. © King Features Syndicate.

Nell Brinkley, "Nell Brinkley Narrative Pages." Drawn for Hearst's *American Weekly* newspaper magazine supplement, Nell Brinkley's color pages started appearing in 1918. They often involved lengthy serial narratives (hence the name they were soon given by readers, although they were given no formal overall title by the author) and were extremely popular with the readers up to the time of their discontinuance, due to the artist's other commitments, in the early 1930s. © Hearst Newspapers.

Grace Drayton, "Dimples." Grace Drayton specialized in features about cute young children of both sexes, and "Dimples" is as good an illustration as any of her somewhat mannered style of drawing. In this 1917 example she chose a more fanciful way of storytelling.

Edwina Dumm, "Cap Stubbs and Tippie." Edwina Dumm (who signed simply "Edwina") specialized in kid and animal features. This charming strip combined both.
© George Matthew Adams Service.

Dale Conner Ulrey, "Mary Worth's Family." Dale Ulrey was the second artist to work on "Mary Worth." She thus bridged the gap between Martha Orr, the strip's creator, and Ken Ernst, its best-known illustrator. © Publishers Syndicate.

Dale Messick, "Brenda Starr." Dale Messick created her renowned comic strip in 1940, and she wrote and drew it (with the help of others) until her retirement in 1980. © Tribune Media Services.

Ethel Hays, "Flapper Fanny." Ethel Hays was an early woman pioneer of the comics. She created the character of Flapper Fanny in the mid-1920s. © NEA Service.

Gladys Parker, "Mopsy." Gladys Parker succeeded Ethel Hays on the "Flapper Fanny" feature which she drew from 1932 to 1938, when she created "Mopsy."
© NEA Service.

Maria Teresa Alzamora, romance comic. Maria Teresa Alzamora is famous for her rendition of Pantera Negra, a Spanish clone of Tarzan, but her forte remained soap opera comics, of which this is a sample. © Ediciones Lumen.

Grazia Nidasio, "Valentina Melaverde." Italian cartoonist Grazia
Nidasio created her best-loved comic strip, "Valentina Melaverde,"
about a dreamy and winsome teenage girl, in 1968. It is still running
to this day, testament to Grazia Nidasio's talent and subtle humor.
© Il Corriere dei Ragazzi.

Lina Buffolente, "Liberty Kid." Lina Buffolente was born in
Vicenza, Italy, in 1924, and was perhaps the first Italian woman
comics artist, beginning in 1942. She soon specialized in the
Western genre, and among her many contributions to this field
"Liberty Kid" is one of the best known. © Casa Editrice Universo.

Ruth Carroll, "The Pussycat Princess." "The Pussycat Princess" was Grace Drayton's last comic strip creation in 1935. Upon her death the following year, the feature was taken over by Ruth Carroll who worked in close imitation of her predecessor's style in these slight tales of the kingdom of Tabbyland, a country peopled by round-faced, exceedingly cute kittens. © King Features Syndicate.

Isabella Bannerman, *et al.,* "Six Chix." The all-women team of "Six Chix" struts its stuff in this feature started in the first month of the year 2000. © King Features Syndicate.

"Women competing in world-class sporting events, women commanding space shuttle missions; Gee, next thing you know there will be equal pay."

" Here comes the new department manager and Brad Pitt look-alike! Quick! Look sexy, yet capable of closing the Walberger account!"

If you experience eyestrain at work, simply focus momentarily on something far away.

HAVE A NICE DAY.

Elena Uzhinova. Elena Uzhinova is that rarity among rarities, a *female* Russian cartoonist. Her comics present a wry commentary on contemporary Russian life and society. © Elena Uzhinova.

Machiko Hasegawa, "Sazae-san." Machiko Hasegawa started a quiet revolution in 1946 with her gently funny family strip "Sazae-san." Following in her footsteps, several generations of female Japanese cartoonists have achieved equal rights (in the world of comics, if not in the real world) with their male counterparts. © Asahi Chimbun.

Angela and Luciana Giussani, "Diabolik." The Giussani sisters created the character of Diabolik, dubbed "the king of terror," in 1962. Despite the outcry of its detractors, "Diabolik" is still going strong, having already survived the death of one of the sisters. © Astorina.

Hilda Terry, "Teena." Hilda Terry is best known for her creation of "Teena," which started appearing as a daily panel titled "It's a Girl's Life" in 1941, later renamed "Teena" for the main character. An endearing and whimsical look at typical American teenage girls of the time, it lasted until 1964. © King Features Syndicate.

Lynda Barry. Born in 1956, Lynda Barry started cartooning during her college years. In addition to *Ernie Pook's Comeek* (formerly *Girls & Boys*), she has continued to draw editorial cartoons, and has produced a number of books. © Lynda Barry

Julie Hollings. Julie Hollings is arguably the foremost underground cartoonist in Britain, and her cartoon stories have appeared in a number of alternative-style magazines. © Julie Hollings.

Maria Pilar Sanchis, "El Cisne Encantado." Born in Zumàrraga, Spain, in 1938, Maria Pilar Sanchis began her career as a comics artist about 1957. She specialized in fairy tales, and her stories have been published in England as well as Spain. © Maria Pilar Sanchis.

Diane Noomin. Diane Noomin was an early contributor to the underground magazine *Weirdo* in the 1970s. In addition to her cartoon stories, she has edited several collections of works by female cartoonists. © Diane Noomin.

Lynn Johnston, "For Better or for Worse." Born in Canada in 1947, Lynn Johnston was the author of three books on child rearing before creating her award-winning newspaper strip in 1979. © Universal Press Syndicate.

Madeline Brogan, "The First Lady." Born in 1952, Madeline Brogan has already had a long career in cartooning. "The First Lady," about Eve in the Garden of Eden was her first effort at a syndicated comic strip. © Madeline Brogan.

Kathryn LeMieux, "Lyttle Women." This short-lived strip was LeMieux's first attempt at syndication. She is now one of the six women cartoonists to work on the "Six Chix" syndicated package. © King Features Syndicate.

Helena Motta, "Moçambique." Helena Motta was one of the first
women cartoonists in Africa. Among her many achievements, she
illustrated (in 1983 with texts by Eduardo Mondlane) "Moçambique,"
a comic book recounting the struggle of liberation in her country.
© Instituto Nacional do Livro e do Disco.

Cabai, "Three Well-Behaved Girls." The three properly brought-up young ladies here give some helpful hints concerning the raising of chickens in their home village. Cabai is the signature of the premier woman cartoonist in Malaysia. © Creative Enterprises.

Aline Kominsky-Crumb. In addition to being famed cartoonist Robert Crumb's wife, Aline Kominsky-Crumb is also a cartoonist of note in her own right. Her caustic comics about marital life with the mercurial Crumb have often been reprinted. © Aline Kominsky-Crumb.

Marie Severin, "Dignifying Science." Marie Severin was one of the many women cartoonists illustrating this humongous comic book devoted to the accomplishments of women scientists. Her subject was Marie Curie, who received the Nobel Prize for the discovery of radium. © Jim Ottaviani.

Lii Hongqun, "Finally Friends." Born in Shandong province, China, in 1967, Lii Hongqun is one of the up-and-coming stars of Chinese cartooning. Her cartoons have been published nationally, and she has won a number of awards, including the Silver Medal in the National Art Exhibition of 1999. © Lii Hongqun.

Bibliography

This selected bibliography includes books dealing with some general aspect of the subject within a larger framework, as well as books and articles directly devoted to this topic. Monographs on a particular feature, character, or cartoonist have been omitted.

I—Books

(On the general subject of comics only books in English are indicated; those volumes in a foreign language deal specifically with women and comics.)

Abel, Robert H., and David Manning White, eds. *The Funnies: An American Idiom.* New York: The Free Press of Glencoe, 1963.

Becker, Stephen. *Comic Art in America.* New York: Simon and Schuster, 1969.

Benton, Mike. *The Comic Book in America.* Dallas, TX: Taylor Publishing, 1990.

Berger, Arthur Asa. *The Comic-Stripped American.* New York: Walker and Company, 1974.

Blackbeard, Bill. *A Century of Comics* (2 vols.) Northampton, MA: Kitchen Sink Press, 1995.

Conti, Thierry, Sophie Le Boulicault-Brunet, Robert Quatrepoint. *L'Image de la Femme à Travers la Bande Dessinée.* Marseille: Bibliothèque Municipale, 1993.

Couperie, Pierre, and Maurice Horn. *A History of the Comic Strip.* New York: Crown, 1968.

Daniels, Les. *Comix: A History of Comic Books in America.* New York: Outerbridge and Dienstfrey, 1971.

Estren, Mark. *A History of Underground Comics.* San Francisco: Straight Arrow Books, 1974.

Gasca, Luis. *Mujeres Fantasticas.* Barcelona: Editorial Lumen, 1969.

Gifford, Denis. *The International Book of Comics.* London: Deans International Publishing, 1984.

Goulart, Ron, ed. *The Encyclopedia of American Comics.* New York: Facts on File, 1990.

Horn, Maurice, ed. *100 Years of American Newspaper Comics.* New York: Gramercy, 1996.

————. *The World Encyclopedia of Comics* (second edition). Philadelphia: Chelsea House, 1998.

Inge, M. Thomas. *Comics as Culture.* Jackson, MS: University Press of Mississippi, 1990.

Lent, John A., ed. *Themes and Issues in Asian Cartooning: Cute, Cheap, Mad and Sexy.* Bowling Green, OH: Bowling Green State University Popular Press, 1999.

————. *Women and Mass Communications: An International Annotated Bibliography.* Westport, CT: Greenwood Press, 1991.

————. *Women and Mass Communications in the 1990s.* Westport, CT: Greenwood Press, 1999.

Lupoff, Richard, and Donald Thompson, eds. *The Comic Book Book.* New Rochelle, NY: Arlington House, 1973.

O'Sullivan, Judith. *The Great American Comic Strip.* Boston: Little, Brown, and Company, 1990.

Reitberger, Reinhold, and Wolfgang Fuchs. *Comics: Anatomy of a Mass Medium.* Boston: Little, Brown, 1972.

Robbins, Trina. *A Century of Women Cartoonists.* Northampton, MA: Kitchen Sink Press, 1994.

————. *From Girls to Grrrlz: A History of Girls' Comics from Teens to Zines.* San Francisco: Chronicle Books, 1999.

—— *The Great Women Superheroes*. Northampton, MA: Kitchen Sink Press, 1996.

Robinson, Jerry. *The Comics: An Illustrated History of Comic Strip Art*. New York: Putnam, 1974.

Sabin, Roger. *Comics, Comix, and Graphic Novels*. London: Phaidon Press, 1997.

Sadoul, Jacques. *L'Enfer des Bulles*. Paris: J.-J. Pauvert, 1968.

—— *Les Filles de Papier*. Paris: J.-J. Pauvert, 1971.

Schodt, Frederik. *Manga! Manga!: The World of Japanese Comics*. New York: Kodansha International, 1983.

Sheridan, Martin. *Comics and Their Creators*. Boston: Hale, Cushman and Flint, 1942.

Steranko, James, ed. *The Steranko History of Comics*. Reading, PA: Supergraphics (2 vols.), 1970 and 1972.

Waugh, Coulton. *The Comics*. New York: Macmillan, 1947.

Wertham, Fredric. *Seduction of the Innocent*. New York: Rinehart and Co., 1954.

II—Articles

(Only articles dealing in some significant way with the subject of women and the comics have been included.)

Amadieu, Georges. "L'Eternel Féminin Triomphe dans les Bandes Dessinées," in *V-Magazine*, Winter 1968, Paris.

Barcus, Francis E. "The World of Sunday Comics," in *The Funnies: An American Idiom*.

Bruggeman, Theodor. "Das Bild der Frau in der Comics.," in *Studien zur Jugendliteratur*, 1956, Hamburg.

Buch, Hans-Christoph. "Sex-Revolte im Comic Strip," in *Pardon*, No. 12, 1966, Munich.

Chambon, Jacques. "Statut de la Femme dans les Bandes Dessinées d'Avant-Garde," in *Mercury*, No. 7, 1965, Paris.

Eisenstodt, Gale, and Kerry Dolan, "Watch Out, Barbie," in *Forbes*, Jan. 2, 1995, New York.

Horn, Maurice. "Défense et Illustration de la Pin-Up dans la Bande Dessinée," in *V-Magazine*, Fall 1965, Paris.

Macek, Carl. "Good Girl Art—An Introduction," in *Comic Book Price Guide* (sixth edition), Cleveland, TN, 1976.

Mareuil, Chantal. "La Femme dans la Bande Dessinée," in *Guida alla Mostra Internazionale dei Cartoonists*, Rapallo, Italy, 1976.

Matera, Fran. "Feminists and the Funnies," in *Editor & Publisher*, Oct. 24, 1987, New York.

Perini, Maria-Grazia. "Sexus Sequior," in *Guida alla Mostra Internazionale dei Cartoonists*.

Saenger, Gerhart. "Male and Female Relationns in the American Comic Strip," in *Public Opinion Quarterly*, Summer 1949, Princeton, NJ (reprinted in: *The Funnies: An American Idiom*).

Snider, Marie. "A Century of Women: Do The Comics Tell the Truth?," paper delivered at the Popular Culture Association meeting, March 18, 1992.

Walker, Mort. "Do Women Have a Sense of Humor?," in *Guida alla Mostra Internazionale dei Cartoonists*.

A Sampler of Women Cartoonists

Consuelo Arizmendi (Sin Patria)

Martine Berthelemy (Ceux de Chibougamau)

Marbel Burvik, under the pseudonym "Odin" (Dickie Dare)

Kate Carew (Handy Andy; The Angel Child)

Ruth Carroll (The Pussycat Princess)

Virginia Clark (Oh Diana!)

Dale Connor (Mary Worth's Family, as half of "Dale Allen")

Bertha Corbett (Sunbonnet Babies)

Fanny Cory (Babe Bunting; Little Miss Muffet)

Isabell Dethan (Tante Henriette)

Grace Drayton (toodles: Dolly Dimples; The Pussycat Princess)

Edwina Dumm under the pseudonym "Edwina" (The
　　Meanderings of Minnie: Cap Stubbs and Tippie

Mary Fleener (Boogie Chillun)

Shary Flenniken (Bonnie an' Trots)

Evelyn Flinders (The Silent Three)

Mary Gauerke (The Alumnae)

Alice Harvey (Sister Susie)

Ethel Hays (Flapper Fanny)

Marjorie Henderson under the pseudonym "Marge" (Little Lulu)

Virginia Huget (Campus Capers)

Tove Jansson (Mumin)

Selby Kelly (Pogo)

Carol Lay (Story Minute)

Marty Links (Bobby Sox; Emmy Lou)

Dale Messick (Brenda Starr)

Tarpe Mills (The Cat-Man; Miss Fury)

Kate Murtah (Annie and Fanny)

Rose O'Neill (The Kewpies)

Martha Orr (Apple Mary)

Kate Osann (Tizzy)

Gladys Parker (Flapper Fanny, Mopsy)

Marie Severin (Doctor Strange; The Hulk;
　　Sub-Mariner)

Carol Swain (The Fire Bug)

Tomoko Taniguchi (Aquarium)

Hilda Terry (Teena)

Liu Xinhua (Disappointed)

Marjorie (Marge) Henderson,
"Steaming Youth." © Marjorie Henderson.

Fanny Cory, "Little Miss Muffet."
© Fanny Y. Cory.

Edwina Dumm, "Tippie." © George Matthew Adams Service.

Virginia Huget, "Campus Capers." © Premier Syndicate.

Martha Orr, "Apple Mary." © Publishers Syndicate.

Rose O'Neill, "The Kewpies."
© Rose O'Neill.

Mary Fleener, "Boogie Chillun!" © Mary Fleener.

The fire Bug

Carol Swain, "The Fire Bug." © Carol Swain.

Consuelo Arizmendi (Spain), "Sin Patria." © Florita.

Liu Xinhua (China), "Disappointed."
© Liu Xinhua.

Tomoko Taniguchi (Japan),
"Aquarium." © Tomoko Taniguchi.

Tove Jansson (Finland), "Mumin." © Bulls Presstjanst.

Carol Lay, "Story Minute." © Carol Lay.

Isabelle Dethan (France), "Tante Henriette."
© Delcourt.

Martine Berthelemy (France), "Ceux de Chibougamau." © Martine Barthelemy.

Evelyn Flinders (England), "The Silent Three." © Amalgamated Press.

Index

CARTOONISTS AND WRITERS

Abdelrrahim, Anissa, 249
Adams, Neal, 169
Aidans, Edouard, 186
Alfieri, Janet, 217, 226
Altan, Francisco Tullio, 197, 211
Alzamora, Maria Teresa, 247, 256
Amor, Tina, 245
Andriola, Al, 83, 127, 156
Arizmendi, Consuelo, 247, 276
Armstrong, Robb, 232
Atkinson, Ruth, 243

Bailey, Ray, 127
Baker, Matt, 12, 151
Balabakki, Fatima, 249
Bald, Ken, 147, 169
Baltus, Anne, 246
Baraou, Anne, 235, 246
Barbara, 247
Barclay, Valerie, 243
Barr, Donna, 245
Barrett, Monte, 54
Barry, Lynda, 194, 202, 245, 263
Barry, Sy, 81
Beck, C. C., 117
Becker, Franziska, 197, 221, 247
Becker, Stephen, 43, 120
Bender, Jack, 107
Bennerman, Isabella, 245, 260
Berthelemy, Martine, 246, 279
Bertram, Moira "Bert," 243
Bess, Gordon, 172
Bilal, Enki, 196
Binder, Jack, 117
Bolle, Frank, 52
Bollen, Roger, 227
Bostwick, Sals, 6
Bradley, Melvin, 146
Brady, Pat, 193, 200
Brahmania, 240
Brandoli, Anna, 197, 212, 246
Brandon, Barbara, 217-218, 224, 245
Brandon, Brumsie Jr., 217
Branner, Martin, 48, 52
Breathed, Berke, 218
Bretécher, Claire, 246
Brewster, Ann, 243
Brewster, Orrin, 218
Briggs, Clare, 31, 51
Brigman, June, 203, 245
Brinkerhoff, Robert Moore, 41

Brinkley, Nell, 252
Brogan, Madeline, 217, 229, 266
Brown, William, 185
Browne, Bob, 157, 167
Browne, Dik, 157
Buck, Frank, 104
Buffolente, Lina, 154, 246, 258
Burvik, Mabel Odin, 243
Buscema, John, 206
Bushmiller, Ernie, 67
Butterworth, Jenny, 162, 186, 245

Cabai, 249, 268
Calkins, Richard, 74, 79, 92
Callahan, Jack, 46
Caniff, Milton, 77, 85, 95, 99, 100, 101, 114, 115, 120, 123, 124, 125, 197
Capp, Al, 78, 83, 107, 115, 141, 149
Carew, Kate, 242
Carey, Ed, 33
Carr, Gene, 19, 27, 32
Carroll, Lee, 60
Carroll, Ruth, 259
Casson, Mel, 156, 185
Cauvin, Raoul, 246
Cestac, Florence, 246
Chaffin, Glen, 73
Cho, Frank, 218, 223
Christman, Bert, 85
Chu, Ronald, 214
Claremont, Chris, 209
Clark, Todd, 228
Clark, Virginia, 242, 243
Cochran, Dot, 242
Cochran, Tony, 218, 224
Cockrum, Dave, 209
Coll, Charles, 91
Colley, Ed, 217, 226
Colon, Ernie, 210
Conner, Dale, 243
Connor, Amanda, 245
Conselman, Bill, 48, 55
Conway, Gerry, 206
Cory, Fanny, 112, 242, 272
Counihan, Bud, 108
Coutts, John Alexander Scott, 163
Craft, Jerry, 218
Crane, Roy, 10, 70, 71, 122
Cravath, Glen, 104
Crepax, Guido, 163, 188, 189, 190
Crouch, Bill, 76
Crumb, Robert, 161, 180, 220
Cullen, Jean, 244

Dale, Barbara, 217

Dallis, Nicholas, 140, 146, 160, 164
Davis, Phil, 95
Dean, Allen, 102
DeBeck, Billy, 36, 72
Delainey, Gary, 225
De la Parra, Guillermo, 249
De Tessier, Isabelle Emilie. See Duval, Marie
Dethan, Isabelle, 246, 278
Dickenson, Steve, 228
Dirks, Rudolph, 20
Dodd, Howell, 85
Doran, Colleen, 220, 245
Doucet, Julie, 220, 238, 245
Drake, Stan, 12, 140, 144, 145
Drayton, Grace, 242, 243, 253, 259
Drechsler, Debbie, 245
Dugmore, Harry, 233
Dumm, Edwina, 243, 253, 272
Durack, Elizabeth, 243
Durack, Mary, 243
Duval, Marie, 241, 250
Dwyer, Bill, 58

Ed, Carl, 57
Edwina, 253
Eisner, Will, 114, 133, 134
Elder, Will, 173
Eliot, Jan, 218, 226, 245
Ellis, Frank, 54
Ernst, Ken, 142, 242, 254
Espinosa, Maria, 249
Evans, George, 98
Evans, Greg, 193, 201

Falk, Lee, 81, 94, 95
Fallon, Sparrow, 134
Feign, Larry, 197, 210
Fernandez, Fernando, 197
Fisher, Ham, 105
Fleener, Mary, 245, 274
Fleming, Sean, 243
Flenniken, Shary, 191
Flinders, Evelyn, 244, 280
Flowers, Don, 243
Forest, Jean-Claude, 162, 182
Forrest, Hal, 73
Foster, Hal, 84
Foster, Harold, 97
Fradon, Ramona, 203, 244, 245
Francis, Stephen, 233
Frazetta, Frank, 141, 149, 150
Fredericks, Harold "Fred," 95
Fuller, Ralph, 75, 106
Fung, Paul, 58

Gaiman, Neil, 227
Gebbie, Melinda, 244
Gellage, Martha, 221, 235
Geller, Ruth, 243
Geniés, Carmen Barbara, 247
Geradts, Evert, 179
Gibbs, Cecilia May, 241
Gifford, Denis, 110, 162
Gillon, Paul, 158
Giussani, Angela, 246, 262
Giussani, Luciana, 246, 262
Godwin, Frank, 48, 50-51, 77, 89, 152
Goetzinger, Annie, 196, 215, 246
Goldberg, Rube, 70
Gotto, Ray, 115, 128
Gould, Chester, 79
Gould, Will, 82, 95
Graff, Mel, 111
Grave, Dave, 107
Gravett, Paul, 196
Gray, Clarence, 75, 86, 87
Gray, Harold, 51, 61
Gregory, Roberta, 220, 236, 244
Griffith, Bill, 194
Gross, Milt, 63
Gutiérrez, Antonio, 249

Haenigsen, Harry, 138
Hagio, Moto, 248
Hamlin, V. T., 107
Hammett, Dashiell, 98
Hancock, Myra, 245
Hasegawa, Machiko, 248, 261
Hays, Ethel, 242, 255
Hayward, A. E., 37, 47
Held, John, 78, 109
Henderson, Marge, 242, 272
Hernandez, Carmen, 249
Hernandez, Gilbert, 196, 207
Hernandez, Jaime, 196, 207
Hérout, Sophie, 246
Herrera, Josefina Diaz, 249
Hershfield, Harry, 36, 40, 41, 51, 64
Hewlett, Jamie, 237
Hoest, Bill, 194, 202
Hogarth, Burne, 76, 84, 115, 118, 119, 138
Holdaway, James, 187
Hollánder, Nicole, 194, 201
Hollander, Sylvia, 245
Hollings, Julie, 196, 264
Hongqun, Lii, 248, 269
Horseman, Mollie, 244
Howard, Greg, 193
Howard, Robert E., 175
Howarth, F. M., 18, 24
Huget, Virginia, 242, 273
Huppen, Hermann, 181

Iessel, Manon, 246
Iger, S. M. "Jerry," 93, 140
Ikeda, Ryoko, 13, 248
Inns, Kenneth, 155

Jansson, Tove, 247, 278
Johnson, Barbara, 204

Johnson, Ferd, 69
Johnston, Lynn, 193, 200, 244, 266

Kahles, Charles William, 25
Kane, Bob, 141, 158, 159, 179
Keaton, Russell, 77, 90
Keefe, Jim, 80
King, Frank, 69
Kirby, Jack, 174
Kitchen, Denis, 161
Kominsky-Crumb, Aline, 220, 268
Koojima, Koo, 162
Kopervas, Gary, 223
Kotzky, Alex, 160, 164
Kotzky, Brian, 164
Kuhn, Charles, 135
Kurtzman, Harvey, 173

Lambert, Nicole, 197
Languereau, Maurice, 29
Lash, Batton, 211
Lasswell, Fred, 72
Lawrence, Jim, 166
Lay, Carol, 245, 278
Lay, Janine, 246
Lazarus, Mel, 153, 178
Lebrun, Denis, 225
LeDoux, Harold, 146
Lee, Stan, 161, 167, 174, 176
Le Mieux, Kathryn, 217, 245, 266
Links, Martha "Marty," 137, 243
Lob, Jacques, 162, 177
Longaron, Jorge, 166
Lubbers, Bob, 141, 147, 160, 165
Lynde, Stan, 154

MacGill, H. A., 42
Machamer, Jefferson, 68
Magni, Enzo, 131
Maki, Miyako, 198, 248
Marcus, Jerry, 177
Mareuil, Chantal, 5-6
Maroto, Esteban, 184
Marrs, Lee, 244
Marschall, Richard, 106, 300
Marston, William, 116
Marten, Hazel, 243
Martin, Edgar, 48, 60
Mayerik, Val, 176
McCay, Winsor, 18, 22
McClure, Darrell, 62, 64
McEvoy, J. P., 54
McGruder, Aaron, 233
McGuire, Jack, 54
McKean, Dave, 227
McMain, Neysa, 243
McManus, George, 8, 19, 28, 35-36, 38, 39
McWilliams, Al, 168
Messick, Dahlia, 243. *See also* Messick, Dale
Messick, Dale, 11, 12, 76, 115, 126, 203, 243, 254
Milgrom, Allen, 208
Miller, Frank, 103, 209
Mills, June, 243. *See also* Mills, Tarpe
Mills, Tarpe, 114, 117, 243

Miralles, Ana, 247
Mishkin, Dan, 210
Mitsuhashi, Chikako, 248
Mitton, Jean-Yves, 221
Miyazaki, Hayao, 198, 234
Mizuno, Hideko, 248
Mohr, Jean, 242
Montana, Bob, 115, 130
Montellier, Chantal, 221, 246
Mooney, Jim, 172
Moore, Dick, 69
Moore, Ray, 81, 94
Mora, Victor, 196, 207
Morgan, Wallace, 30
Morrow, Gray, 84
Mosley, Jack, 103
Motta, Helena, 249, 267
Munson, Cecilia Paddock "Pad," 243
Murphy, Jimmy, 66
Murphy, John Cullen, 97
Myers, Russ, 170

Nidasio, Grazia, 246, 257
Nolan, Graham, 146
Noomin, Diane, 245, 265
Norris, Paul, 86, 87
Nowlan, Phil, 79, 92

O'Brien, Kath, 243
Odoi, Frank, 221
O'Donnell, Peter, 187
O'Neill, Harry, 99
O'Neill, Rose, 242, 243, 251, 273
Opper, Frederick Burr, 18, 22
Ormes, Jackie, 76, 112, 243
Orr, Martha, 242, 254, 273
Oshima, Yumiko, 248
Outcault, Richard Felton, 18, 21
Overgard, Bill, 149

Pad, 243
Paley, Nina, 193
Parker, Gladys, 7, 12, 50, 55, 217, 242, 243, 255
Patenaude, Ramona "Pat," 243
Patterson, Alicia, 243
Patterson, Russell, 3, 148
Pattinger, Colette, 246
Pellaert, Guy, 162, 183
Pellos, René, 138
Perry, Bill, 69
Peter, H. G., 116
Peters, Mike, 203
Pett, Norman, 78, 110
Piccolo, Rina, 245
Pichard, Georges, 162, 177
Pinchon, J. P., 29
Pini, Richard, 244
Pini, Wendy, 244
Piro, Stephanie, 245
Plumb, Charles, 48, 55
Pran, 197
Pratt, Hugo, 197
Prentice, John, 122
Price, Garrett, 105

Price, Hilary, 245
Puchol, Jeanne, 235, 246

Queirolo, Renato, 212

Rasmussen, Gerry, 225
Rausch, Barbara, 196, 215, 245
Raymond, Alex, 72, 75, 80, 96, 97, 98, 115, 121, 122, 140
Raymond, James, 136
Ritt, William, 86, 87
Robbins, Frank, 75, 85, 134
Robbins, Trina, 161, 191, 196, 207, 217, 244, 245
Robertson, Jennifer, 244
Robinson, Paul, 65
Romera, Enrique, 187
Romita, John, 176
Ross, Charles Henry, 241, 250
Ross, Penny, 34
Ross, Russell, 54
Rudahl, Sharon, 244
Rusz, Livia, 247
Ryan, T. K., 168

Sadler, Marilyn, 227
Salinas, José-Luis, 148
Sanchis, Maria Pilar, 247, 264
Satonaka, Machiko, 248
Saunders, Allen, 106, 142, 160, 242
Saunders, John, 168
Scancarelli, Jim, 69
Schacheri, Rico, 233
Scheuer, Chris, 197
Schmich, Mary, 203
Schmidt, Charles, 81
Schodt, Frederik, 197
Schoenke, Bob, 54
Schultze, Sydney, 198
Schulz, Charles, 153
Segar, E. C., 37, 45, 68, 109
Segura, Antonio, 247
Severin, Marie, 244, 269
Shannon, Dink, 14
Shuhui, Wang, 248
Shulock, Margaret, 245
Shuster, Joe, 88
Shutian, Guo, 248
Sickles, Noel, 75, 85
Siegel, Jerome, 88
Sienkiewicz, 209
Simmonds, Rosemary "Posy," 196, 245
Sinnott, Joe, 172
Sio, Enric, 162
Skelly, Hale, 166
Skelly, Jerry, 166
Slate, Barbara, 245
Smith, Sydney, 44
Smythe, Reg, 171
Snider, Marie, 194
Sparling, Jack, 118
Springer, Jack, 167
Stamm, Russell, 131
Stanton, Eric, 163
Starr, Leonard, 12, 140, 143, 204

Sterrett, Cliff, 37, 43
Striebel, John, 54
Sullivan, Eddie, 81
Swain, Carol, 275
Sylvere, Jean, 138

Takahashi, Rumiko, 197, 198, 213, 248
Takeuchi, Naoko, 221, 248
Taniguchi, Tomoko, 277
Tardi, Jacques, 196
Telnaes, Ann, 245
Terry, Hilda, 129, 243, 263
Terry, John, 85
Thomas, W. Morgan, 93
Thorne, Frank, 175
Tourret, Pat, 162, 186, 244
Tourtel, Mary, 241, 250
Townsend, Inez, 242
Trudeau, Gary, 161, 165
Tsuchida, Yoshiko, 248
Tufts, Warren, 129, 152
Tuthill, Harry J., 43

Ulrey, Dale Conner, 254
Ulrey, Herb, 243
Uppal, Jagjit, 240
Urfer, Dorothy, 242
Uzhinova, Elena, 247, 261

Valle, Jo, 33
Vallet, André, 33
Van Bibber, Max, 52
Van Buren, Ray, 83
Vargas, Yolanda, 249
Verback, Gustave, 19, 26
Villagran, José, 230
Voight, Charles, 5, 42, 50-51, 60

Walker, Mort, 10, 157, 205
Walsh, Brandon, 51, 62
Walter, Jerry, 243
Walter, Linda, 243
Watanabe, Masako, 248
Waugh, Coulton, 43, 243
Webb, Robert, 93
Weber, Bob, 171
Wendling, Claire, 246
Wertham, Frederic, 140
Westover, Russ, 48, 50, 53
Whedon, Joss, 220, 231
Wheelan, Ed, 49-50, 56
Whitman, Bert, 115, 132
Wiederseim, Grace, 242
Willard, Frank, 69
Willington, C. H., 40
Wilshire, Mary, 245
Wilson, Ron, 175
Wilson, W. O., 31
Wilson, Woody, 146
Woggon, Bill, 196, 215
Woggon, Elmer, 106, 196
Wolfman, Marv, 175
Wolinski, George, 162
Wood, Wally, 193
Wooley, Pat, 245

Wright, David, 155
Wunder, George, 123

Xiaoyuan, Liu, 248
Xinhua, Liu, 248, 277

Yamagishi, Ryoko, 198
Yamamoto, Sumika, 198
Young, Dean, 136, 225
Young, Lyman, 72
Young, Murat "Chic," 50, 58, 72, 78, 136
Yunzhi, Mao, 248

Zangele, Peggy, 243

COMICS

Abbie n' Slats, 76, 83
Abie the Agent, 36, 41
Ace McCoy, 150
Ada, 197, 211
Adam, 194
Adèle Blanc-Sec, 196
Adventures of Kathryn, The, 36
Affairs of Jane, The, 50
Agnes, 218, 224
Alley Oop, 107
Ally Sloper, 241, 250
Amethyst, Princess of Gemworld, 210
Andy Capp, 6, 171
Angel Child, The, 242
Annibelle, 242
Annie, 204. See also Little Orphan Annie
Anti Bwalo, 221, 235, 249
Apartment 3-G, 160, 164
Apple Mary, 142, 242. See also Mary Worth
Aquaman, 244
Aquarium, 277
Archie, 130
Arlo n' Janis, 194
Aurore, 246
Ayer, Lane, 243

Babe Bunting, 112
Baby Blues, 194
Bahadur and Bela, 240
Barbarella, 162, 182
Barney Baxter, 103
Barney Google, 72
Barney Google and Snuffy Smith, 72
Batman, 179, 244
Beautiful Bab, 50, 72
Beetle Bailey, 141, 205, 219
Ben Casey, 169
Beryl the Bitch, 196
Betty, 4-5, 50-51, 60, 225
Betty Boop, 108
Bib and Bub, 241
Big Chief Wahoo, 106, 149
Blanche Epiphanie, 162, 177
Blondie, 78, 111, 136, 225
Bloom County, 218
Bobby Socks, 137, 243
Boob McNutt, 70

Boogie Chillun, 274
Boondocks, The, 233
Boots and Her Buddies, 48, 50, 60
Brenda Starr, 8, 11, 76, 115, 126, 243, 245, 254
Brick Bradford, 75, 86, 87
Bring 'em Back Alive, 104
Bringing Up Father, 8, 35, 38
Broncho Bill, 99
Broom Hilda, 170
Buck Rogers, 74, 77, 79, 92
Buffy, the Vampire Slayer, 220, 231
Bungle Family, The, 43
Buster Brown, 18, 21
Buz Sawyer, 122

Calamity Jane, 246
California Girls, 196
Calvin and Hobbes, 194
Campus Capers, 242
Cap Stubbs and Tippie, 253
Captain Kate, 160-161, 166
Carmencita, 247
Carol Day, 155
Casey Ruggles, 129
Cat, The, 244
Cathy, 192-193, 199, 244
Cellulite, 246
Ceux de Chibougamau, 279
Charlie Chan, 76, 83
Cinderella Peggy, 42
Cinderella Suze, 46
Cisco Kid, The, 148
Claire Voyant, 114, 118
Cloak and Dagger, 195
Color Blind, 218
Conan the Barbarian, 176
Connie, 8, 48, 50-51, 59, 77, 89
Corto Maltese, 197
Couple, The, 214

Danny Dreamer, 31
Dateline: Danger!, 168
Deathless Deer, 243
Debbie Dean, Career Girl, 115
Dennis the Menace, 141
Desert Peach, The, 245
Desparate Desmond, 36, 40, 51, 64
Diabolik, 246-247, 262
Dickie Dare, 243
Dick Tracy, 79
Dignifying Science, 269
Dimples, 253
Dirty Plotte, 220, 238
Disappointed, 277
Distant Soil, A, 220, 245
Dixie Dugan, 48, 49, 54
Doctor Srange, 244
Dolly Drake and Bobby Blake, 242
Dolly of the Follies, 49
Don Proverbio, 249
Don Winslow, 76
Doonesbury, 6, 161, 165
Drago, 115, 118
Dr. Kildare, 169
Dumb Dora, 48, 50, 58, 242

Durga Rani, 138

Easy Edgar, 242
Eipuron Obasan, 248
El Cisne Encantado, 264
Elfquest, 244
Ella Cinders, 48, 55
Elvira, Mistress of the Dark, 230
Emmy Lou, 137, 143
Ernie Pook's Comeek, 194, 202, 263
Etta Kett, 50
Eva Medusa, 247

Fantastic Four, The, 161, 174
Félina, 196, 215, 246
Finally Friends, 269
Fiordistella, 246
Fire!, 248
Fire Bug, The, 275
First Lady, The, 217, 229, 245, 266
Flameman, 243
Flamingo, 140-141, 151
Flapper Fanny, 12, 55, 242, 255
Flash Gordon, 80, 96
Flyin' Jenny, 77, 90, 217. 243
For Better or For Worse, 193, 200, 244, 266
For This We Have Daughters?, 37
Francie, 194
Friday Foster, 160, 166
Frisco Jim, 246
Fritzi Ritz, 48, 67
Furio, Mascherato, 246

Gags and Gals, 68
Gasoline Alley, 69
Girls and Boys, 194, 200
Gretchen Gratz, 242
Gumnut Babies, 241
Gumps, The, 35, 44
Gus and Gussie, 49, 66

Hagar the Horrible, 167
Hairbreadth Harry, 25, 36
Haphazard Helen, 36
Happy Hooligan, 22
Harold Teen, 50, 57, 115
Hazards of Helen, 36
Hazel the Heartbreaker, 42
Heart of Juliet Jones, The, 140, 144, 145, 158
Hello Carol, 204
Hello Hattie, 6
Hi and Lois, 157, 219

Ijuwaru Basan, 248
Il Piccolo Ranger, 246
In the World of Wonderful Dreams, 22
I Testamenti di Sant' Ambrogio, 212, 246
It's a Girl's Life, 129, 243, 263
It's Me, Dilly!, 156

Jackson Twins, The, 159
Jane, 78, 110
Jane, Daughter of Jane, 110
Jane Arden, 48, 49
Jane Calamity, 154

Jo and Her Magic Cape, 243
Jodelle, 162, 183
Joe Palooka, 105
Johnny Comet, 141, 150
Johnny Hazard, 134
Joyah Sport, 249
Juba II: Roi des Maures, 249
Judd Saxon, 147
Judette Camion, 246
Judge Parker, 140, 146
Julie Bristol, 246
JumpStart, 232
Jungle Jim, 97

Katzenjammer Kids, The, 20
Kerry Drake, 127
Kewpies, The, 242, 243, 251, 273
Kid Sister, The, 72
King of the Royal Mounted, 102

Lady Bountiful, 19, 27
Lance, 152
La Strega, 246
Les Déblok, 246
Les Frustrés, 246
Les Gnan-Gnan, 246
Les Naufragés, 246
Les Panthéres, 186
L'espiègle Lili, 33
Les Triplés, 197
L'Histoire d'O, 190
Liberty Kid, 246, 258
Liberty Meadows, 218, 223
Li'l Abner, 107, 141, 149
Little Annie Fanny, 163, 173
Little Mary Mixup, 41
Little Miss Muffet, 112
Little Nemo, 18, 22
Little Nemo in Slumberland, 22-23
Little Orphan Annie, 61, 163, 204
Lola, 228
Long Sam, 141, 147
Love and Rockets, 196
Love Life of Harold Teen, The, 57
Luann, 193, 201
Luther, 217
Lyttle Women, 217, 245, 266

Madam and Eve, 221, 233
Mahiru Lullaby, 198
Maison Ikkoku, 197, 213, 248
Male Call, 114, 120
Mama's Boyz, 218
Mamie, 148
Mamma's Angel Child, 34
Mandrake the Magician, 95
Marianne, 242
Marvin, 194
Mary Noticias, 247
Mary Perkins, 143. See also On Stage
Mary Worth, 139, 142, 160, 254
Me and My Boyfriend, 242
Medusa, 198
Meet Misty, 196, 207
Merely Margy, 78, 109

Mighty Isis, 173
Millie the Model, 243
Minute Movies, 49, 56
Miracle Jones, 119
Miss Peach, 153
Mixed Singles, 185
Mocambique, 267
Modesty Blaise, 162, 187
Molly the Manicure Girl, 242
Momma, 178
Moon Mullins, 69
Moose, 171, 218
Moose and Molly, 218
Mopsy, 7, 55, 242, 255
Mother Goose and Grimm, 203
Mr. and Mrs., 51
Mumin, 247, 278
Myra North, Special Nurse, 91

Naughty Bits, 220, 236
Nausicaa of the Valley of Wind, 198, 234
Nevada Jones, 243
Newlyweds, The, 19, 28, 34, 51
Newlyweds and their only child, The, 28
Nize Baby, 51, 63
Nungalla and Jungalla, 243

Oaky Doaks, 75, 106
Oh, Diana, 243
Olly of the Movies, 49
On Stage, 140
Outland, 218
Out on a Limb, 223
Ozark Ike, 128

Pam, 244
Pantera Bondi, 131
Pantera Negra, 247, 256
Pa's Son-in-Law, 36, 40
Patsy, 111
Patsy Walker, 243
Paulette, 162
Peanuts, 6, 141, 153
Penny, 138
Perils of Pauline, The, 36, 51
Petey, 42
Petey Dink, 42
Petting Patty, 68
Phantom, The, 81, 94
Phantom Lady, 12
Phyllis, 32
Pinkerton Jr., 81
Polly and Her Pals, 37, 43
Positive Polly, 43
Prince Valiant, 71
Puck: The Comic Weekly, 4
Pussycat Princess, The, 243, 259

Radio Patrol, 76, 81
Ranma 1/2, 198, 248
Red Barry, 76, 82, 95
Redeye, 172
Red Prince, The, 243
Red Sonja, 245
Rex Morgan, M.D., 140, 146

Rhymes with Oranges, 245
Rick O'Shay, 154
Rilhat Ibn Battuta, 249
Rip Kirby, 115, 121, 122, 140
Robin Malone, 160, 165
Rose Is Rose, 193, 194, 200
Rose of Versailles, 248
Rosie's Beau, 35, 39
Rumic World, 248
Rupert the Bear, 241, 250
Rusty Riley, 152

Sabrina, the Teenage Witch, 220
Safe Havens, 194
Sailor Moon, 221, 248
Sallie Slick and her Surprising Aunt Amelia, 242
Sallie Snooks, Stenographer, 14
Sally Forth, 193, 194, 199
Sazae-san, 248, 261
Scarlet O'Neil, 131
Scarth, 162
Scorchy Smith, 75, 85
Secret Agent X-9, 98
Sheena, Queen of the Jungle, 93, 140
Show Girl, 49, 54
Silent Three, The, 244, 280
Simon Simple, 33
Sin Patria, 276
Skull Valley, 105
Skyroads, 74
Smilin' Jack, 103
Snookums, 28
Somebody's Stenog, 37, 47
South Sea Girl, 140-141, 151
Spider-Man, 176
Spirit, The, 133, 134
Stanley Family, The, 217, 245
Steaming Youth, 272
Steve Canyon, 115, 124, 125
Steve Roper, 149
Stone Soup, 218, 226, 245
Story Minute, 278
Sub-Mariner, 244
Suburban Cowgirl, 217, 226
Superman, 76, 88, 155, 244
Supernatural Law, 211
Susie Q. Smith, 243
Sweet Gwendoline, 163
Sylvia, 194, 201

Tailspin Tommy, 73
Tales of Durga, 239
Tank Girl, 237
Tante Henriette, 278
Tarzan, 76, 79, 84
Ted Towers, Animal Master, 104
Teena, 129, 243, 263
Terry and the Pirates, 77, 99, 100, 101, 115, 123
Thimble Theater, 37, 45, 68, 109
13 Rue de l'Espair (13 Hope Street), 140, 158
Three Well-Behaved Girls, 268
Thun'da, 141, 150

Tiffany Jones, 8, 162, 186, 245
Tiga Dara Pingitan, 249
Tillie the Toiler, 48, 49, 53, 199
Tippie, 243, 272
Toodles, 242
Toots and Casper, 51, 66
Torchy Brown, 243
Torchy in Heartbeats, 112
Trudy, 177
True Love, 196
Tsuruhime Ja!, 248
Tumbleweeds, 168
Turr'ble Tales of Kaptain Kiddo, The, 242
2's Kompeni, 249

Upside Downs of Little Lady Lovekins and Old Man Muffaroo, 19, 26

Vae Victis, 221
Valentina Melaverde, 246, 257
Vanilla and the Villains, 51, 64
Vesta West, 127
Vickie Valentine, 196, 215
Virtue of Vera Valiant, The, 161, 167

Wanda the War Girl, 243
Wash Tubbs, 10, 70, 71
Where I'm Coming From, 217, 224
White Boy, 105
Wimmen's (Wimmin's) Comix, 191, 220, 244
Winnie Winkle, 48, 49, 52
Wolff, 184
Wolff & Byrd, Counselors of the Macabre, 211
World of Lily Wong, The, 210

Xena: Warrior Princess, 220, 230
Xi Xiang Ji, 248
X-Men, 208, 209

Yellow Kid, The, 17
Young Love, 243

Zenon—Girl of the 21st Century, 222, 227
Zora y los Hibernautas, 197

FICTIONAL COMICS CHARACTERS

Abadab, Gussie, 49, 66
Abie (*Abie the Agent*). *See* Kabibble, Abie
Ada (*Ada*), 197, 211
Adèle Blanc-Sec, 196
Adolphus, 177
Agatha Crumm, 194, 202
Agnes (*Agnes*), 218, 224
Alane (*South Sea Girl*), 151
Aleta, Queen of the Misty Isles, 77, 97
Alley Oop, 107
Amethyst, Princess of Gemworld, 195, 210
Anderson, Gwen, 221, 233
Andrews, Archie, 115, 130
Andrews, Cathy, 192-193, 199

Andy Capp. *See* Capp, Andy
Angelica, 162
Annie Fanny, 163, 173
Anti Bwalo, 235
Apple Mary, 142, 242. *See also* Worth,
  Mary
Archibald (*Rosie's Beau*), 39
Archie. *See* Andrews, Archie
Ardala. *See* Valmar, Ardala
Arden, Dale, 75-76, 77, 80
Arden, Jane, 54
Aunt Fritzi. *See* Ritz, Fritzi
Auranella, 162

Babe Bunting, 242
Bahadur, 240
Baker, Lucy, 148
Banshee, 197
Barbarella, 162, 182
Barbie, 220
Barb Wire, 219
Barnes, Betty Lou, 73, 74, 76
Barney Google, 72
Barrow, Kirk, 83
Barry, Red, 77, 82
Batgirl, 141, 159, 179
Batman, 114, 141, 158, 159, 179, 195
Batson, Mary Bromfield, 114. *See also*
  Marvel, Mary
Batwoman, The, 141, 158, 159
Baxter, Barney, 103
Beautiful Bab, 72
Bécassine, Caumery, 29
Bela, 240
Bêlit, 176
Betty (*Archie*), 115, 130
Betty (*Betty*), 51, 60, 225, 242
Betty Boop, 108
Betty Lou (*Tailspin Tommy*). *See* Barnes,
  Betty Lou
Bianca, 189
Bioskop, Jill, 196
Black Canary, 219
Black Fury, 114, 243. *See also* Miss Fury
Blake, Betty, 102
Blinks, Belinda, 18-19, 25, 36, 51
Blondie, 6, 78, 111, 136, 219, 225
Blossom, Phyllis, 69
Bodicea, 221
Boopadoop, Blondie. *See* Blondie
Boots, 50, 60
Bouche Dorée, 197
Bradford, Brick, 86, 87
Brandy (*Liberty Meadows*), 218, 223
Bristol, Julie, 221
Broncho Bill, 99
Broom Hilda, 6, 170
Buffy, 220
Bumstead, Alexander, 136
Bumstead, Blondie. *See* Blondie
Bumstead, Cookie, 136
Bumstead, Dagwood, 111, 136
Bungle, George, 43
Bungle, Jo, 43
Burma, 77, 78, 101

Burnem, Bobbie, 149
Buster Brown, 21
Byrd, Alanna, 211

Calhoun, Copper, 115, 124
Camion, Judette, 235
Cantrell, Owen, 144
Canyon, Poteet, 115, 125
Canyon, Steve, 115, 124, 125, 160
Capp, Andy, 171
Capp, Flo, 6, 171
Captain Easy, 113
Captain Kate, 166
Captain Marvel, 114, 117
Captain Marvel Jr., 114
Carol (*Hello Carol*), 204
Cathy (*Cathy*). *See* Andrews, Cathy
Caucus, Joanie, 6, 161, 165
Charlie Brown, 153
Charlie Chan, 113
Chouka, 186
Chris (*Casey Ruggles*), 129
Cinderella Peggy, 42
Cinderella Suze, 46
Cinders, Ella, 49, 55
Cinders, Lotta Pill, 49
Cinders, Mytie, 49
Cinders, Prissie, 49
Cisco Kid, 148
Claire Voyant, 114, 118, 195
Cobb, Joe, 232
Cobb, Marcy, 232
Cobb, Sunny, 232
Colby, Mercedes, 76
Colt, Denny, 133. *See also* Spirit, The
Comanche, 181
Conan the Barbarian, 161, 176, 184
Connie (*Connie*). *See* Kurridge, Constance
Constance (*Danny Dreamer*), 31
Countess, The, 71
Custer, Catherine, 104

Daddy Warbucks, 61
Dagger, 195
Dagwood. *See* Blumstead, Dagwood
Daisy Mae, 6, 78, 107, 115, 141
Dale, Jane, 72
Dale, Trixie, 72
Danvers, Carol, 172, 195. *See also* Ms.
  Marvel
Danvers, Linda Lee, 141. *See also* Supergirl
Dare, Dick, 56
Dare, Jenny, 77, 90
Daredevil, 195, 209
Day, Carol, 155
Day, Molly, 76, 81
Dean, Debbie, 115, 132
Deare, Hazel, 50
Death, 219, 227
Deering, Wilma, 75, 76, 79
Defendar, 177
Der Captain, 17
Desperate Desmond, 36, 40
De Vrille, Lil', 77, 97
Die Mamma. *See* Mamma Katzenjammer

Dillon, Darlene, 226
Dilly, 156
Dinah (*Ozark Ike*), 115, 128
Dirty Plotte, 238
Doctor Fate, 219
Dolan, Ellen, 133
Donnerwetter, Gus, 66
Doonesbury, Michael J., 165
Dora Bell, 50, 58, 111
Dorian, Honey, 115, 121, 122
Drago, 118
Dragon-Lady, The, 77-78, 99
Drake, Kerry, 127
Drake, Lefty, 127
Drake, Marla, 114. *See also* Miss Fury
Drake, Normandie, 77, 78, 100
Driver, Sam, 146
Dugan, Dixie, 49, 54, 55
Dumb Dora. *See* Dora Bell
Durge, 239
Durga Rani, 138

Éclair, Claude, 36, 40
Elektra Natchios, 195, 209
Elvira, 230
Emmy Lou, 137
Epiphanie, Blanche, 177
Eve (*The First Lady*), 229

Fallon, Sparrow, 134
Feitelbaum, Isidore, 51
Feitelbaum, Ma, 51, 63
Félina, 196, 215
Feminax, 221
Flagston, Chip, 157
Flagston, Ditto, 157
Flagston, Dot, 157
Flagston, Hi, 157
Flagston, Lois, 157, 219
Flagston, Trixie, 157
Flame, The, 77, 95
Flamingo, 140, 151
Flapper Fanny, 50, 55, 255
Flash Gordon, 75, 76, 77, 96
Flo (*Andy Capp*). *See* Capp, Flo
Fluffy Ruffles, 30
Forth, Hillary, 193, 199
Forth, Sally, 193, 199
Forth, Ted, 193, 199
Foster, Friday, 166
Fracas, Hal, 56
Francoise (*Les Panthères*), 186
Freddie the Sheik, 50
Fumble, Phil, 67

Gale (*Smilin' Jack*), 103
Gale, June, 6, 140, 146
Gay Abandon, 154
Ghost, 219
Goldberg, Lenore, 161, 180
Google, Barney, 72
Gordon, Barbara, 179
Graingerfield, Vanilla, 51, 64
Grandma, 135
Granny (*Out on a Limb*), 223

Great Gusto, The, 106
Gretchen (*Dr. Kildare*), 169
Grimm, 203
Grimm, Ben, 174
Grits, 127
Groggins, Becky, 76, 83
Gumbo, Jimbo, 193, 200
Gumbo, Rose, 193, 200
Gump, Andy, 44
Gump, Minerva "Min," 35, 44
Gussie (*Gus and Gussie*). *See* Abadab, Gussie

Hairbreadth Harry. *See* Hollingsworth, Hairbreadth Harry
Hamhacker, Hildegard, 168
Happy Hooligan, 18
Harold Ham Gravy, 37, 45, 109
Hazard, Johnny, 134
Hobbs, Francis, 178
Hobbs, Mary Lou, 178
Hollingsworth, Hairbreadth Harry, 18, 25
Honi (*Hagar the Horrible*), 167
Hopey, 196
Hotsy Totsy, 50
Howe, Ann, 105
Hyster, 91

Ibn Battuta, 249
Ingrid the Bitch, 161
Invisible Girl, 161, 174

Jackson, Jean, 159
Jackson, Jill, 159
Jackson, Robin, 168
Jameson, Christy, 122
Jameson, J. Jonah, 172
Jane (*Jane*), 78, 110
Jane (*Tarzan*), 84
Jane Calamity, 154
Jazmine, 233
Jean (*Johnny Comet*), 150
Jiggs, 35, 38, 51
Jodelle, 183
Joker, 195
Jones, Eve, 140, 145, 158
Jones, Juliet, 6, 12, 140, 144, 145, 158, 160
Jones, Tiffany, 186
Judge Parker, 140
Jungle Jim, 77, 97, 113

Kabibble, Abie, 36, 41
Kane, April, 123
Kane, Killer, 77, 92
Keene, Katy, 196
Kent, Clark, 76, 88. *See also* Superman
Kett, Etta, 50, 65
Kewpies, 251
Kholderup, Wilbur, 196
King (*King of the Royal Mounted*), 102
King Morpheus, 18
Kirby, Rip, 115, 121, 122
Kurridge, Constance, 51, 59, 77, 115

Lady Jaguar, 134

Lady Justice, 219
Lady Luck, 114
Lafitte, Lilli, 129
Lai-Lah, 184
Lane, Gina, 76, 83, 91
Lane, Jack, 91
Lane, Lois, 76, 88, 91
Lane, Margo, 91
Leander, 18, 24
Lee, Pagan, 122
Lieutenant Sharpnell, 24
Li'l Abner, 78, 107, 141, 149
Lili (*L'espiègle Lili*), 33
Little Annie Rooney, 51, 62
Little Egypt, 69
Little Lady Lovekins, 19, 26
Little Lulu, 242
Little Miss Muffet, 112, 242, 272
Little Nemo, 18
Little Orphan Annie, 51, 61, 204
Lodge, Veronica, 115, 130
Lois (*Hi and Lois*). See Flagston, Lois
Lola (*Lola*), 228
Long Sam, 141, 147
Lovewell, Lillums, 50, 57
Luann, 201
Lucy (*Peanuts*). See Van Pelt, Lucy
Lugg, Sgt. Louise, 219
Lulu (*Lulu and Leander*), 18, 24
Luthor, Lex, 195

Ma (*Pa's Son-in-Law*), 40
Mabel (*Petey*), 42
Madge, the Magician's Daughter, 18, 31
Magee, Margo, 160, 164
Maggie (*Bringing Up Father*), 35, 38, 51
Maggie (*Love and Rockets*), 196, 207
Malone, Robin, 165
Mama (*Mama's Boyz*), 218
Mamie (*Mamie*), 148
Mamma (*Mamma's Angel Child*), 34
Mamma Katzenjammer, 17, 20
Mandrake, 77, 95
Marcy (*JumpStart*), 232
Margy (*Merely Margy*), 109
Marie Jade, 197
Marlys, 202
Marshall, Maxine "Max," 226
Martin, Smilin' Jack, 103
Marvel, Mary, 114, 117
Mary-Jane (*Buster Brown*), 18, 21
Maura (*Barney Baxter*), 103
McCoy, Kitty, 72
McKay, Marion, 179
McSneer, Ralph, 56
McSpade, Angelfood, 161, 180
McSwine, Moonbeam, 141, 149
Messalina, 162
Mews, Autumn, 134
Mickey (*Scorchy Smith*), 85
Mighty Isis, 173, 195
Miles, Patti, 152
Miller, Molly, 171
Miller, Moose, 171
Mills, Peggy, 74

Min (*The Gumps*). *See* Gump, Minerva
Mindy (*Kerry Drake*), 127
Ming the Merciless, 76, 96
Minnie Ha-Cha, 106
Miss Buxley, 205
Miss Fury, 114, 117
Mississippi (*Red Barry*), 76, 82
Miss Lace, 114-115, 120
Miss Peach, 153
Miss Peachtree, 33
Misty (*Meet Misty*), 207
Modesty Blaise, 162, 187
Momma (*Momma*), 178
Moonbeam McSwine. *See* McSwine, Moonbeam
Mopsy, 255
Morel, Francoise, 140, 158
Morgan, Rex, 140, 146
Mother Goose, 203
Mr. Fantastic, 174
Mrs. Hobbs, 178
Mrs. Newlywed, 28
Ms. Marvel, 172, 195, 206
Muffet, Milly, 112
Mullins, Moon, 69
Murdoch, Matt, 209

Nancy (*Fritzi Ritz and Nancy*), 67
Natacha, 197
Nausicaa of the Valley of Wind, 198, 234
Nell (*Broncho Bill*), 99
Nicki (*Ben Casey*), 169
Nora (*Bringing Up Father*), 35, 36, 38
North, Myra, 77, 91

O, 190
Oaky Doaks, 106
O'Day, Darby, 115, 118
Old Man Muffaroo, 19
O'Neil, Scarlet, 131
Onthespot Charley, 24
Olive Oyl. *See* Oyl, Olive
Olson, Summer, 115, 124
Oola (*Alley Oop*), 107
O'Shay, Rick, 154
Otonashi, Kyoko, 197, 213
Oyl, Castor, 37, 45, 68
Oyl, Cylinda, 68
Oyl, Olive, 37, 45, 68, 78, 109
Ozark Ike, 115, 128

Palmer, Diana, 75, 76, 81
Palooka, Joe, 105, 113
Pantera Bionda, 131
Pantera Negra, 256
Parker, Peter, 176
Patsy (*Patsy*), 111
Patterson, April, 193
Patterson, Elizabeth, 193
Patterson, Elly, 193, 200
Patterson, John, 193
Patterson, Michael, 193
Pearl (*Boob McNutt*), 70
Pearlman, Reba Mine Gold, 36, 41
Peggy (*Judd Saxon*), 147

Penny (*Penny*). *See* Pringle, Penelope
Perkins, Mary, 12, 140, 143
Perkins, Maw, 37
Perkins, Paw, 37
Perkins, Polly. *See* Positive Polly
Petting Patty, 68
P'Gell, 134
Pha, 141, 150
Phantom, The, 75, 76, 77
Phantom Lady, 10
Phyllis (*Phyllis*), 32
Polly. *See* Positive Polly
Popeye the Sailor, 78, 109
Porter, Pauline, 218
Positive Polly, 37, 43
Powers, Grace, 98
Powers, LuAnne, 160, 164
Powers, Tarleton, 98
Pravda, 183
Prince, Diana, 113. *See also* Wonder Woman
Prince Barin of Arboria, 96
Princess Aura, 77, 96
Princess Leecia, 84
Princess Narda, 77, 95
Princess of Slumberland, 18, 22-23
Prince Valiant, 78, 97
Pringle, Penelope, 138
Professor Papagoras, 164
Professor Zarkov, 80
Professor Zero, 91
Pryde, Kitty, 195, 208

Queen Fria, 96

Raven, 195
Raven, Danny, 168
Raven, Wendy, 168
Rebecca (*I Testamenti di Sant' Ambrogio*),
    197, 212, 246
Red Dust, 181
Red Sonja, 161, 175, 176
Richards, Reed, 174
Richards, Susan, 161, 174
Riley, Rusty, 152
Ritz, Fritzi, 67
Robin (*Batman*), 141
Rogers, Buck, 75, 76, 92
Rogue, 195
Roper, Steve, 149
Rosamond (*Desparate Desmond*), 36, 40, 51
Rose (*Rose Is Rose*). *See* Gumbo, Rose
Rosie (*Rosie's Beau*), 35-36, 39
Rosselli, Valentina, 188
Rossendale, Rudolph, 18, 19, 25
Rota, 87
Rouge, Blanche, 50, 56
Rox, Lorelei, 134
Ruckett, Rodney, 58

Ruggles, Casey, 129
Ryan, Pat, 78, 99, 100, 101, 123

Sailor Moon, 221
St. John, Basil, 126
St. Lorne, Lance, 152
Sala, 77, 94
Salisbury, June, 86
Salisbury, Van Atta, 86
Sallie Snooks, 14
Sandhurst, Normandie Blake, 77, 78, 100
Sandhurst, Tony, 78
Satin, Silk, 134
Sawyer, Buz, 122
Saxon, Judd, 147
Scarth, 162
Scraggs, Daisy Mae. *See* Daisy Mae
Scrapple, Slats, 83
Segrid (*Mandrake*), 95
Seminova, Marina, 197
Sheena, Queen of the Jungle, 12, 77, 93, 131
She-Hulk, 194
Shimatiji, 197
Simple, Simon, 33
Sisulu, Eve, 221, 233
Skeeter, 73
Smilin' Jack. *See* Martin, Smilin' Jack
Smith, Ronald-Ann, 218
Smith, Scorchy, 75, 85, 113
South Sea Girl, 140, 151
Spencer, Abbey, 146
Spider-Man, 176
Spider-Woman, 175, 194
Spirit, The, 133, 134
Stacy, Gwendolyn, 176
Starfire, 195
Starlight, 105
Starr, Brenda, 12, 115, 126, 132, 160, 203
Stella Mix, 185
Stenog, The, 47
Stone, Alix, 218
Stone, Holly, 218
Stone, Val, 218, 226
Storm, 195, 209
Storm, Johnny, 174
Sugardaddy Bigbucks, 163, 173
Supergirl, 141, 155
Superman, 76, 88, 113, 141, 155
Suzanne (*Happy Hooligans*), 18, 22
Sybil (*Tarzan*), 84
Sylvia (*Sylvia*), 194, 201
Syncopating Sue, 50

Taffy (*Emmy Lou*), 137
Tailspin Tommy, 73, 76
Tango, 70
Tank Girl, 196, 337
Tarzan, 113

Tawney (*Redeye*), 172
Teena (*Teena*), 129, 263
Terry (*Terry and the Pirates*), 78, 99, 113, 123
Thomas, Andrea, 173, 195
Thompson, Tommy, 160, 164
Tillie the Toiler, 49, 53, 78, 192
Toots (*Toots and Casper*), 51, 66
Tootsie, 219
Torchy Brown, 76, 112
Towers, Ted, 104
Tracy, Dick, 75, 115
Trevor, Steve, 113
Troy (*Dateline: Danger!*), 168
Trudy (*Trudy*), 177
Trueheart, Tess, 75, 76, 79
Tsukino, Usagi, 221
Tumbleweed, 168

Uranella, 162

Valentina, 163, 188
Valentine (*Les Panthères*), 186
Valiant, Vera, 167
Valmar, Ardala, 77, 92, 94
Vampirella, 161
Vampire Queen, 97
Vanilla. *See* Graingerfield, Vanilla
Van Pelt, Lucy, 6, 153
Veronica (*Archie*). *See* Lodge, Veronica
Virginia "Ginny" (*Doonesbury*), 161

Wahoo, 106
Walkuriax, 221
Wallet, Walt, 69
Washington, Martha, 219
Wash Tubbs, 70, 71
West, Vesta, 127
White, Pearl, 36
White Boy, 105
Williams, Kathryn, 36
Winkle, Perry, 49
Winkle, Winnie, 49, 52, 78, 192
Wisp O'Smoke, 134
Witch Hazel, 119
Wonder Woman, 12, 113, 114, 116, 195
Wong, Lily, 197, 210
Worth, Mary, 6, 142, 144, 218, 242

Xena, 220
X-9, 98, 113

Young, Theodore Randolph Oscar "Troy,"
    168

Zatanna, 219
Zatara, 219
Zenon, 227
Zora (*Scorchy Smith*), 85